THE BOOK OF

MALAYSIAN
COOKING

THE BOOK OF
MALAYSIAN
COOKING

HILAIRE WALDEN

Photographed by
SIMON BUTCHER

HPBooks

ANOTHER BEST SELLING VOLUME FROM HP BOOKS

HPBooks
Published by The Berkley Publishing Group
200 Madison Avenue
NewYork, NY 10016

9 8 7 6 5 4 3 2 1

ISBN 1-55788-289-4

By arrangement with Salamander Books Ltd.

Home Economist: Lucy Miller
Printed and bound in Spain by Bookprint, S.L.

CONTENTS

INTRODUCTION 7

MALAYSIAN INGREDIENTS 8

EQUIPMENT 11

SOUPS 12

STARTERS & SNACKS 18

FISH 30

POULTRY 43

MEAT 53

NOODLES & RICE 62

VEGETABLES 71

VEGETARIAN DISHES 79

ACCOMPANIMENTS 85

DESSERTS 92

INDEX 96

FOREWORD

Malaysian cuisine is a fusion of the different cooking styles and dishes of three nationalities – Indian, Chinese and indigenous Malay. These have merged to make a unique, harmonious blend that is an identifying characteristic of the charming style and taste of the food of this tropical peninsula.

The Indians contributed spices such as cumin, turmeric and chiles, and their art of blending spices is reflected in the many Malaysian curries. Indian-style flat-breads, chutneys and relishes frequently accompany meals. The Chinese presence is evident in the use of soy sauce, hoisin sauce, spring rolls and stir-fries. The Chinese influence is particularly strong in Singapore. In the 1820s many thousands of Chinese laborers flocked to Singapore to work on the construction of the city. Through intermarriage with Malay women, a clearly identifiable race of Nonya (or Straits Chinese) resulted, who practice a style of cooking that combines the Chinese emphasis on texture and balance of tastes with the Malaysian predilection for curries and chile dishes. As the north of the Malaysian peninsula borders with Thailand, a definite Thai flavor can be detected in the use of lemon grass, coriander and galangal. The many years of Portuguese, Dutch and British occupation have also left their mark on Malaysian cooking.

Malaysian cuisine is a very healthy one. Chicken is the most widely eaten meat. With a large Muslim population and a significant number of Hindus, pork and beef are not used to any great extent. Besides, the climate is not conducive to rearing livestock for eating. Fish and seafood are plentiful and widely eaten. Rice is the staple food, while noodles are also used to bulk out meat dishes, to thicken soups and generally add substance to the diet. Both rice and noodles are also popular as snacks.

Desserts are light and refreshing. A Malaysian meal does not usually include a dessert beyond, perhaps, some of the tropical fruits such as mangoes, lychees, pineapples, rambutans and star-fruit that grow in profusion. Coconut palms thrive, so coconut is a predominant ingredient. Coconut milk provides the liquid in many of the country's curries, and the national soup, Laksa Lemak (see page 12), is made from coconut milk, prawns (or sometimes chicken), lemon grass, lime juice, coriander and chiles. Coconut milk is also the basis of desserts such as coconut custard.

Preparation and cooking techniques are simply those used in the West or by Chinese and Indian cooks. Malaysian food is served and eaten informally. Dishes are placed in the center of the table and diners help themselves, using chopsticks for food of Chinese origin, or a spoon and fork, or the fingers of the right hand, for Indian-style food. Banana leaves are used for eating rice or to serve as plates.

MALAYSIAN INGREDIENTS

Candlenuts Creamy colored waxy nuts that are used to add thickness and texture to curries and casseroled dishes. Raw macadamia or cashew nuts can be substituted.

Chiles A very important feature of Malaysian cooking, and used in large amounts, not only for their hotness and flavor, but also for their thickening quality. Some supermarkets now sell specific varieties of chiles, and label them to show the degree of hotness, but if there is no indication of hotness, smaller varieties are invariably hotter than large ones.

Dried chiles, which are always red, have a more earthy, fruity flavor, and fresh green chiles have a "greener", less rounded flavor than red ones, which are riper. The seeds and white veins inside a chile are not only hotter than the flesh, but have less flavor, and are generally removed before cooking. Chiles contain an oil that can irritate the eyes and skin, so avoid touching your eyes and mouth when preparing chiles and always wash your hands when you have finished handling them.

Chinese black mushrooms These dried mushrooms have a pronounced flavor and must be soaked for 20–30 seconds before use. The stalks tend to be tough so are usually discarded. Dried black mushrooms vary in quality and thickness; choose the thickest, which are usually also the most expensive.

Choi sum Similar to pak choi, but smaller, with narrower stalks, slightly paler green leaves and yellow flowers.

Coconut cream The layer that forms on the top of coconut milk when it is left to stand. It is usually added almost at the end of cooking.

Coconut milk This is not the liquid that comes from a coconut, but is made by soaking coconut flesh in hot water. To make coconut milk from fresh coconut, put the shredded flesh from a medium coconut in a bowl, pour 1¼ cups boiling water over and leave to soak for 30 minutes. Pour into a sieve lined with cheesecloth

and press hard to extract as much liquid as possible.

To make coconut milk from unsweetened dried shredded coconut, put 2⅔ cups in a blender, pour in 1¼ cups very hot water and mix for 1 minute. This milk tends to be richer than milk made from fresh coconut. Ready prepared coconut milk is sold in cans and plastic pouches. It sometimes has a thicker consistency than home-made coconut milk. Once cool, coconut milk should be kept in the refrigerator. It may separate on standing; either spoon off the thick layer and use as coconut cream or stir it back into the milk. When thin coconut milk is called for in a recipe, use milk from which cream has been removed.

Creamed coconut Sold in hard white blocks, which should be kept in a cool place or the refrigerator. Creamed coconut can be used to make coconut milk – grate or chop 3oz. and dissolve in 1¼ cups hot water – or it can be added, after grating or chopping, straight to the hot cooking liquid in a pan towards the end of cooking.

Curry leaf A small, dark green leaf used in some dishes of southern Indian origin.

Dried shredded coconut This is sometimes dry-fried and pounded. Heat it in a small, heavy skillet over medium-high heat until lightly darkened with a roasted aroma. Cool slightly, then pound in a mortar and pestle, or in a small bowl using the end of a rolling pin.

Fish sauce Used in Southeast Asia much as soy sauce is used in China, fish sauce is a thin, salty brown liquid made from salted shrimp or fish. It adds a very special flavor, which is not fishy, to dishes.

Galangal A member of the ginger family. The flavor is distinctive, rather more earthy than ginger but in a subtle way. Dried galangal can be bought, both as a powder and in slices, but if you are unable to get fresh galangal it is better to substitute ginger root.

Garlic An important flavoring in Malaysian cooking. Local garlic cloves tend to be smaller than those sold in Western countries.

Kaffir lime leaves Dark green, highly aromatic leaves with a clean citrus-pine smell and flavor. Kaffir lime leaves freeze well, laid flat in a heavy-duty plastic bag. Use the grated peel of ordinary limes if kaffir leaves are not available, substituting 1½ teaspoons for 1 kaffir lime leaf.

Lemon grass This delicious fragrant, lemony (though not sour) herb is known as serai in Malaysia. To use, cut off the root tip and top end to leave the lower 4–6 inches or so, peel away the tough outer layers then thinly slice the inner part. Even when ground in a blender, it needs to be sliced quite thinly first or else it does not grind properly. To prevent drying out, store with the end in a little cold water. Lemon grass also freezes well. To defrost, hold briefly under running hot water. The grated rind of ¼ lemon can be substituted for 1 lemon grass stalk.

Noodles Both fresh and dried Chinese egg noodles in a variety of different widths are used in Malaysia, but in the West fresh noodles can be quite difficult to come by. They may be found packed in plastic bags in the refrigerated section of Chinese grocery stores. Chinese dried egg noodles are often in bundles or 'nests', which should be shaken loose before using. Some Chinese dried egg noodles are soaked before use. Others are cooked like dried pasta, by dropping into a saucepan of boiling water. Some varieties cook very quickly, so test frequently. See also Rice stick noodles.

Oils Vegetable oil is used when the taste is not a part of a recipe. Peanut oil is used for its characteristic flavor.

Oyster sauce A thick brown sauce made from oysters cooked in soy sauce, then mixed with seasonings. It is not fishy, but richly meaty.

Pak choi Also known as bok choi, this is a type of cabbage that has a slightly bulbous base and long leaves that have white stalks and ribs topped by dark green leaves. The stalks have a mild, refreshing flavor and the leaves taste pleasantly tangy and bitter. It is best cooked quickly to retain

From top to bottom: Coconut milk, Galangal, Lemon grass, Green chiles, Fresh noodles, Curry leaves, Kaffir lime leaves, Garlic, Candlenuts, Fresh noodles, Red chiles, Pak choi.

both the flavor and texture. Pak choi is available in many supermarkets, but if you are unable to find it use Chinese leaves or spinach.

Palm sugar A delicious honey-colored, raw sugar much used in Malaysia. It is sold in lump and free-flowing forms in cans and plastic packages in Malaysian and Thai food shops. Light brown sugar is an adequate substitute.

Rice The staple food of Malaysia. A number of different types are used but the most popular is fragrant long-grain rice, usually imported from Thailand. This is now becoming widely available in the West. Basmati rice, with its long, thin grains and nuttier flavor, is sometimes called for in Indian recipes. Ordinary long-grain rice can be substituted for both types.

Rice stick noodles (rice vermicelli) These thin, brittle and semi-transparent noodles are sold in bundles. For most uses the noodles are soaked before cooking, but when they are served crisp they are used dry.

Rice wine The most common rice wine is Shao-Hsing. It is whiskey-colored and has a rich, sweetish flavor. Dry sherry may be substituted.

Sesame oil Asian sesame oil is made from roasted sesame seeds so is dark in color and has a delicious, rich nutty flavor. Because the flavor is quite pronounced, the oil is used only in small amounts, rather like a seasoning. Sesame oil is sold in small bottles that should be stored in the dark in a cool place, but not the refrigerator as the oil will become cloudy.

Shallots A red variety is commonly found in Malaysia. They are used in large amounts instead of onions, and are included as part of a spice paste.

Shrimp, dried These are used throughout Southeast Asia so can be bought from any of the region's ethnic shops. They are sold in clear plastic packages, which allow you to check that the shrimp are a good pinkish color. They need to be soaked in hot water for 10–15 minutes and are usually ground before use. Keep them in an airtight container in a cool place.

Shrimp paste Known as belaccan (pronounced blachan) in Malaysia but more often found elsewhere as trasi or blachan, the Indonesian and Burmese names. It is made from fermented shrimps, dried and pounded to a paste, and used in small amounts. It is always cooked before use. It may be ground to a paste with other flavorings, or it may be toasted, grilled (broiled) or fried: break off the amount you need and either hold it in tongs over a gas flame, turning it so it roasts evenly, or spread it on a piece of foil and broil it. Alternatively, wrap it in foil and cook it in a dry skillet until it is crumbly and smells fragrant. Raw shrimp paste has a strong smell so keep it in a tightly covered jar; the smell disappears on cooking. In Nonya cooking, black shrimp paste – a black, syrupy seasoning, is used.

Soy sauce Malay cooks use Chinese soy sauces. Light (sometimes known as thin) soy sauce is thinner, paler in color and saltier than dark (thick) soy sauce, which is heavier, sweeter and has a more rounded flavor.

Tamarind This has a distinctive fruity/lemony sharpness. It is found in Asian grocers, peeled, seeded and wrapped in square package. The pulp should be soaked in hot water for about 3 hours then strained through a fine sieve to extract as much liquid as possible. It is the liquid, referred to as tamarind paste, that is used. As a rough guide, use 4oz. tamarind to 1 cup water. Ready-prepared tamarind paste is available.

Turmeric A rhizome similar to ginger, though smaller and more delicate in appearance. It is usually used fresh in Malaysia. It is available fresh in Indian shops but in the West is more usually used ground; ½ teaspoon ground turmeric is equivalent to 1 inch fresh. Fresh turmeric needs to be peeled before use.

Vinegars Chinese white rice vinegar appears in some Malay dishes. It has a mild, delicate flavor. Chinese black vinegar is thicker than most vinegars and has a distinctive rich, spicy fragrance that is similar to balsamic vinegar though sharper. It is used sparingly as a seasoning.

EQUIPMENT

Mortar and pestle Traditionally used for pulverising soft ingredients such as chiles and shallots, as well as crushing spices. It is easier and quicker to use a spice grinder, small blender or special small bowl attachment with a processor for dry spices; for soft foods, use a food processor or blender.

Rice cooker With rice as the staple food, many Malaysian households have electric rice cookers; they make the task of cooking rice easy and they free all the burners on the cooktop.

Wok Widely used in Malaysia for cooking, especially for Chinese-inspired dishes. Thin tempered carbon steel or iron ones are best for heat distribution. Woks made of light stainless steel or aluminium tend to scorch and do not withstand the required heat well. Nonstick surfaces are more expensive but they cannot be heated to sufficiently high temperatures. Electric woks also usually do not heat to high enough temperatures and tend to be too shallow. A wok should be fairly deep with sloping sides so that food falls back into the pan while stir-frying. Because of its shape, flames can encircle a wok and allow it to heat quickly and efficiently. It is the ideal shape for stir-frying as foods can be vigorously tossed around in it. As they touch nothing but well-heated surface, they cook quickly and retain their moisture at the same time. A sauté pan, which is deeper than a skillet, is the best alternative. A wok is also very useful and economical for deep-frying because it will hold a good depth of oil – and less than needed in a straight-sided pan. It can also be used for simmering and steaming.

From top to bottom: Galangal powder, Tamarind, Dried shrimps, Turmeric, Basmati rice, Fragrant long grain rice, Shallots, Palm sugar, Soy sauce, Pestle and mortar

To season a new wok (except a nonstick one) rub it with a dish detergent and rinse well to remove the oil applied at the factory. Put the wok over a low heat. Add 2 tablespoons vegetable oil and wipe it over the sides using paper towels. Heat the wok slowly for 10 minutes then wipe it thoroughly with clean paper towels. Repeat the process three or four times, then wash it in hot water and wipe dry. To clean, simply rinse with hot water after use; with time it will become more and more "nonstick".

Wok accessories
◆A wok stand is needed to hold a wok steady on a gas burner, and to allow the hot air to circulate freely underneath. The best stands are made of wire.
◆A wok lid, usually made from aluminium is useful when making slow-cooking casserole-type dishes that need to be covered. Any large, domed lid that fits snugly on the wok can be used instead, or the wok can simply be covered closely with aluminium foil.
◆A long handled metal spatula shaped like a small shovel is ideal for scooping and tossing food when stir-frying in a wok.

LAKSA LEMAK

3 dried red chiles, cored, seeded and chopped
3 cloves garlic, crushed
6 shallots, chopped
1 (2-inch) piece of ginger root, chopped
1 tablespoon ground coriander
1½ teaspoons ground turmeric
4oz. thin rice noodles
2 tablespoons vegetable oil
1½ lbs. boneless, skinless chicken breasts, cubed
2 cups chicken stock
1 lb. raw, unpeeled medium shrimp
8oz. tofu, cut into ½-inch cubes
8oz. bean sprouts
2 cups coconut milk
Small bunch scallions

Soak chiles in 3 tablespoons hot water in a blender for 10 minutes. Add garlic, shallots and spices; grind to a paste. Soak noodles in hot water for 3-5 minutes, stirring occasionally. Drain. In a wok or saucepan over medium heat, heat oil. Stir in spice paste and cook for 3-4 minutes. Add chicken and cook, stirring, for 3-4 minutes. Add stock; simmer gently for 20-25 minutes.

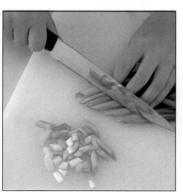

Add shrimp and simmer for 3-4 minutes until they turn pink. Add tofu, bean sprouts, noodles and coconut milk. Stir and simmer for 5 minutes. Thickly slice scallions on diagonal, including some green. Add half to pan. Serve garnished with remaining scallions.

Makes 6 servings.

——PENANG HOT-SOUR SOUP——

1 (8-oz.) whole fish such as trout
5 cups fish or chicken stock
4-5 dried red chiles, cored, seeded and chopped
6 shallots, chopped
1 stalk lemon grass, chopped
3 slices galangal, chopped
1 teaspoon shrimp paste
1 tablespoon paprika
¼ teaspoon ground turmeric
15 fresh mint leaves
1 teaspoon brown sugar
1 teaspoon vegetable oil
3 tablespoons tamarind paste (see page 10)
8oz. dried rice noodles
Salt

In a saucepan, put fish and stock. Cover and simmer for 15 minutes. Lift fish from pan. When cool enough to handle, remove flesh from skin and bones. Return bones to pan and simmer gently, uncovered, for 15 minutes, then strain. Mash fish. Put chiles and 4 tablespoons hot water in a blender; soak for 10 minutes. Add shallots, lemon grass, galangal, shrimp paste, paprika and turmeric. Mix to a smooth paste. Add to pan with strained stock.

Add mint, sugar, oil, tamarind and 1 cup water. Simmer, uncovered, for 15 minutes. Add fish and simmer for 30 minutes. Soak noodles in hot water for 15 minutes, until soft; drain. Cook in boiling salted water for 1 minute; drain. Put in warmed soup bowls. To serve, top with shredded lettuce, fine strips fresh pineapple and cucumber, finely chopped shallots, thinly sliced red chile, mint leaves mixed together.

Makes 3 to 4 servings.

WONTON SOUP

3 oz. boneless, skinless chicken
3 oz. lean pork
3 oz. Chinese sausage
3 oz. peeled shrimp
1 onion, chopped
1 carrot, chopped
1 celery stalk, chopped
6 water chestnuts
2 tablespoons soy sauce
1 tablespoon sesame oil
30 wonton wrappers
7½ cups chicken stock
2 oz. snow peas
1 carrot, cut into fine strips

Dice ¼ of chicken, pork, sausage and shrimp. Set aside. Put remaining chicken, pork, sausage and shrimp in a food processor. Add onion, carrot, celery, water chestnuts, soy sauce and sesame oil. Process to a smooth paste.

Spoon a little of the meat paste on to center of each wonton wrapper. Lightly moisten edges and draw them together to make small packages. In a large saucepan, bring stock to a boil. Add wontons in batches. Return to a boil and simmer for 4-5 minutes. Add snow peas, carrot strips and reserved meats and shrimp. Return to a boil and simmer for a further 4-5 minutes.

Makes 6 servings.

——CHICKEN & NOODLE SOUP——

6oz. thin rice noodles
8oz. boneless, skinless chicken breast
2½ cups chicken stock
2½ cups coconut milk
½oz. tamarind paste (see page 10)
½oz. ginger root, grated
1 stalk lemon grass, very finely chopped
3 tablespoons shrimp paste, toasted (see page 10)
7oz. raw, peeled medium shrimp
3oz. bean sprouts
3oz. peeled, seeded and chopped cucumber

Cook noodles in boiling water for 3-4 minutes. Drain and refresh under running cold water. Drain very well and set aside.

In a saucepan, put chicken and stock. Bring to a simmer and poach for 8 minutes. Lift chicken from stock (reserve stock). When cool enough to handle, shred and set aside. Add coconut milk to pan, with tamarind, ginger, lemon grass and shrimp paste. Bring to a boil then simmer for 5 minutes.

Add shrimp. Simmer for 3-4, then add bean sprouts and cucumber. Heat through for 1-2 minutes. Serve with small dishes of fried onion rings, sliced chiles and cilantro leaves. Serve accompanied by Spicy Sauce (see page 85).

Makes 4 to 6 servings.

—SEAFOOD & COCONUT SOUP—

3 stalks lemon grass, cut into 2-inch lengths
1 (2-inch) piece of galangal, thinly sliced
1 (1-inch) piece of ginger root, thinly sliced
2 teaspoons finely chopped red chile
4½ cups coconut milk
10 kaffir lime leaves
7oz. boneless, skinless chicken breast, cut into
    1-inch cubes
5 tablespoons fish sauce
Juice of ½ lime
7oz. raw unpeeled jumbo shrimp, peeled and
    deveined
7oz. firm white fish fillets, cut into 1-inch cubes
Small handful each cilantro and Thai basil leaves
Cilantro springs, to garnish

In a saucepan, put lemon grass, galangal, ginger and chile. Add 2 cups water. Bring to a boil then simmer for 5 minutes. Add coconut milk and lime leaves. Simmer for 10 minutes. Add chicken, fish sauce and lime juice to pan. Poach for 5 minutes. Add shrimp and fish. Poach for a further 2-3 minutes until shrimp turn pink.

Add cilantro and basil to pan. Stir, then ladle into warm soup bowls. Remove and discard lemon grass and lime leaves before eating. Garnish with cilantro.

Makes 4 servings.

TOFU SOUP

4 cups well-flavored vegetable stock
8oz. tofu, cut into ½-inch cubes
1 fresh red chile, cored, seeded and finely chopped
6 shallots, finely chopped
1 small carrot, finely chopped
2 scallions, sliced into rings
4 tablespoons light soy sauce
2 teaspoons light brown sugar
Salt

Pour stock into a saucepan. Add tofu, chile, shallots, carrot, scallions, soy sauce and sugar.

Bring to the boil, uncovered. Stir briefly then simmer for 2-3 minutes.

Add salt to taste. Ladle the soup into warmed soup bowls. Serve as part of a main meal to counterbalance hot dishes.

Makes 4 servings.

CURRY PUFFS

1 cup unsalted butter
4 cups all-purpose flour
Salt
3 tablespoons vegetable oil plus extra for deep-frying
4 shallots, thinly sliced
2 cloves garlic, finely crushed
1 teaspoon grated ginger root
1 fresh green chile, cored, seeded and finely chopped
4 teaspoons curry powder
1 lb. ground beef, lamb or chicken
1 potato, finely diced
1 tablespoon lime juice, or to taste
6 tablespoons chopped celery leaves
Celery leaves, to garnish

Melt butter with 2 tablespoons water.

In a bowl, combine butter mixture with flour, pinch of salt and about 6 tablespoons water to give a medium-soft dough. Transfer to a work surface and knead for about 10 minutes. Form into a ball. Brush with oil and put in a plastic bag. Leave for at least 30 minutes.

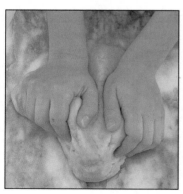

Heat oil in a skillet. Add shallots and fry for 4-5 minutes until browned. Stir in garlic, ginger, chile and curry powder for 30 seconds. Add meat. Cook until pale, stirring to break up lumps. Stir in potato, lime juice, salt to taste and 2 tablespoons water. Simmer gently, covered, for 15-20 minutes until meat and potatoes are tender.

Add celery leaves and cook for 2 minutes. If necessary, increase heat and boil to drive off excess moisture, stirring. Knead dough. Break off a 1-inch piece. Form into a smooth ball then roll to a 4-inch disc.

Put 2 teaspoons meat mixture along center. Brush half of edges of dough circle with water and fold dough over filling.

Pinch edges together to seal. Place, pinched end up, on a plate. Repeat with remaining filling and dough. Heat enough oil for deep-frying in a wok or deep-fryer over medium-low heat. Add a few curry puffs so they are not crowded and fry slowly until golden; turn them over so they cook evenly. Remove with a slotted spoon and drain on paper towels. Serve warm, garnished with celery leaves.

Makes about 30.

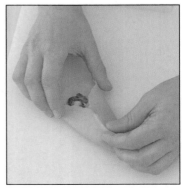

SHRIMP BALLS

1½ lbs. raw, unpeeled jumbo shrimp
1 clove garlic, chopped
1½ tablespoons fish sauce
½ teaspoon light brown sugar
2 teaspoons peanut oil
1 tablespoon cornstarch
1 egg, beaten
Salt and freshly ground black pepper
1½ oz. shredded coconut
2 tablespoons dried breadcrumbs
Cilantro sprigs, to garnish
Dipping Sauce or Spicy Sauce (see page 85)

Reserve 8 shrimp in their shells. Peel remaining shrimp.

With the point of a sharp knife, cut a slit along the back of each peeled shrimp. Remove and discard black intestinal thread. Put shrimp in a food processor. Add garlic, fish sauce, sugar, oil, cornstarch, egg, salt and pepper. Mix to a smooth paste. Transfer to a bowl, cover and chill for 1½ hours.

Preheat broiler. On a baking sheet, combine coconut and breadcrumbs. Wet the palms of your hands; roll the shrimp mixture into 1-inch balls. Coat balls in coconut mixture. Thread on oiled, long metal skewers, adding a reserved shrimp to each skewer. Broil, turning occasionally, for about 6 minutes until balls are firm and whole shrimp are pink. Garnish and serve with dipping sauce of your choice.

Makes 8 servings.

SHRIMP OMELET

6 eggs
1 teaspoon fish sauce
2 teaspoons light brown sugar
1 tablespoon peanut oil
3 oz. bamboo shoots, finely chopped
1 clove garlic, finely chopped
1 teaspoon grated ginger root
2 scallions, including a little green, thinly sliced
2 tablespoons chopped fresh cilantro
6 oz. shelled cooked shrimp
Cilantro sprigs, to garnish

In a medium bowl, beat eggs with fish sauce and sugar. Set aside.

In a wok or skillet heat ½ of oil. Add bamboo shoots, garlic, ginger and scallions. Fry for about 2 minutes. Remove pan from heat and stir in cilantro and shrimp. Add to egg mixture and stir together. In a skillet, heat remaining oil. Stir egg mixture then pour evenly over bottom of pan. Lower heat and leave to cook until underside is set and golden brown and top is almost set.

Put a warm plate upside down on pan. Invert the pan and plate together so the omelet falls onto plate. Using a spatula, slide omelet back into pan and cook until underside is brown. Cut into wedges and garnish with cilantro sprigs.

Makes 3 to 4 servings.

MALAYSIAN SPRING ROLLS

5oz. boneless, chicken breast
4oz. raw shrimp in shell
2 tablespoons peanut oil
1 (½-inch) piece of ginger root, grated
1 clove garlic, finely crushed
3 shallots, very finely chopped
1 small carrot, grated
1 celery stalk, very finely chopped
1 fresh red chile, cored, seeded and finely chopped
2 scallions, chopped
1 teaspoon sesame oil
2 teaspoons soy sauce
12 spring roll wrappers
1 egg, beaten
½ cup vegetable oil

Skin and finely chop chicken. Peel and finely chop shrimp. In a wok or sauté pan, heat peanut oil. Add chicken and stir-fry until beginning to turn opaque. Stir in shrimp and continue to stir-fry until shrimp begin to turn pink. Add remaining ingredients except wrappers, egg and vegetable oil, and fry for 1 minute. Transfer to a bowl and leave until cold.

Spread 1 spring roll wrapper on the work surface; keep remaining wrappers between 2 damp tea towels. Put 1-2 tablespoons filling on lower half of wrapper.

Fold bottom corner up and over filling. Moisten side corners with beaten egg. Fold sides over to cover bottom corner and filling. Press firmly to seal. Moisten top corner with beaten egg.

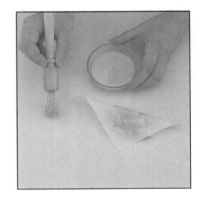

Roll wrapper over tightly to make a neat cylinder. Press top corner to roll to seal. Place seam side down and cover with a damp towel. Repeat with remaining wrappers and filling.

In a wok or sauté pan, heat vegetable oil. Fry rolls in batches for 3-5 minutes, turning occasionally, until golden and crisp. Remove with a slotted spoon and drain on paper towels. Keep warm while frying remaining rolls. Serve with Dipping Sauce (see page 85).

Makes 6 servings.

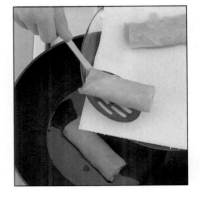

POH PIAH

2 tablespoons vegetable oil
4 shallots, finely chopped
2 cloves garlic, crushed
1 fresh red chile, cored, seeded and finely chopped
4oz. lean pork, ground
4oz. crabmeat
8 water chestnuts, finely chopped
4oz. bamboo shoots, shredded
1 tablespoon light soy sauce
1½ tablespoons salted yellow beans
1 package spring roll wrappers
Spicy Sauce (see page 85)

About 115g (4 oz. each of the following:
Small shrimp
Chinese sausages, steamed and sliced
Bean sprouts, blanched
Scallions
Crisp lettuce leaves, shredded
Cucumber, chopped and coarsely grated

For the filling, in a wok or skillet, heat oil. Add shallots, garlic and chile. Cook, stirring occasionally, until softened and transparent. Stir pork into pan and stir-fry until it changes color. Add crabmeat, water chestnuts, bamboo shoots, soy sauce and yellow beans.

Stir ingredients together for about 2 minutes until well mixed. Leave to cool. Put the cooled meat mixture and the remaining ingredients in individual bowls. Each person helps himself to filling ingredients then rolls up the wrapper, tucking in the ends, and eats it at once. Serve with Spicy Sauce and other accompaniments.

Makes 12.

SPICY SPARE RIBS

3 lb. spare ribs, trimmed and divided into ribs
4 tablespoons vegetable oil
2 scallions, thinly sliced
MARINADE
1 (1-inch) piece of ginger root, grated
4 cloves garlic, finely crushed
1 fresh red chile, cored, seeded and finely chopped
3 tablespoons rice vinegar
⅓ cup dark soy sauce
2 tablespoons peanut oil
1 tablespoon light brown sugar
1 teaspoon Chinese five-spice powder

To make marinade, whisk ingredients together. Put ribs in a dish and pour marinade over.

Turn ribs to coat in marinade, cover and refrigerate for 2-3 hours, turning occasionally. Lift ribs from marinade. Pat dry. Reserve marinade. In a wok or sauté pan, heat oil over high heat. Add 3-4 ribs and cook, stirring, for 2-3 minutes until evenly browned. Using tongs, transfer to paper towels. Repeat with remaining ribs.

Pour off all but 2 tablespoons oil from the pan. Return ribs to pan. Add reserved marinade and enough water to completely cover ribs. Bring to a boil. Lower heat, cover and simmer gently for about 1 hour, stirring occasionally, until meat is tender and shrinks slightly from bone. Boil until cooking liquid is reduced to a thick sauce. Transfer ribs to warmed plates and spoon a little sauce over each serving. Sprinkle with sliced scallions.

Makes 6 servings.

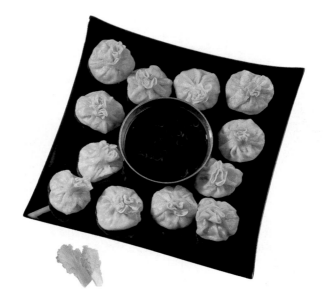

DIM SUM

2¼ cups all-purpose flour
1 cup ground pork
3 scallions, 1 reserved for garnish, 2 chopped,
  including some green
2 large Chinese cabbage leaves, shredded, plus extra
  leaves for lining steamer basket
1 (1-inch) piece of ginger root, grated
1 tablespoon cornstarch
1 tablespoon each light soy sauce and rice wine
2 teaspoons dark sesame oil
½ teaspoon sugar

Sift flour into a bowl. Make a well in center
and slowly pour in 1 cup boiling water. Mix in
flour with a fork or chopsticks.

Continue to mix to form a rough dough,
adding more flour, if necessary. Cover bowl
and leave for 1 minute, to cool. Using your
hands, form dough into a soft, loose ball.
Knead on a lightly floured surface for about
5 minutes until smooth and elastic. Cover
and leave to rest for 30 minutes. In a bowl,
combine remaining ingredients using
chopsticks or a fork. Set aside.

Divide dough in half. Roll each half to a 9-
inch cylinder. Using a floured sharp knife,
cut each cylinder into 12 thick slices. Cover
with a damp cloth.

Roll each slice into a ball then roll out to a 4-inch circle, making edges slightly thinner than center. Place 1 tablespoon filling in center. Brush edges of circle with a little water.

Lift wrapper around filling, gathering and pinching wrapper to form a purse shape. Put on a tray and cover with a damp cloth. Repeat with remaining dough and filling.

Place some dim sum in a steamer basket lined with cabbage leaves, without crowding dim sum. Cover with a lid. Steam over simmering water for 12-15 minutes until tender but chewy. Garnish with reserved scallion and serve warm with soy sauce mixed with shredded fresh red chile for dipping.

Makes 6 to 8 servings.

NONYA PACKAGES

4 dried Chinese black mushrooms
8oz. boneless, skinless chicken breast, thinly sliced
   into strips
1 tablespoon oyster sauce
1½ teaspoons rice wine
1½ teaspoons sesame oil
1 (½-inch) piece of ginger root, grated
1½ teaspoons light soy sauce
1 clove garlic, finely crushed
½ fresh red chile, cored, seeded and finely chopped
2 scallions, including some green, chopped

Soak mushrooms in 3 tablespoons hot water
for 30 minutes. Drain. Discard stems and
finely slice caps.

In a bowl, mix chicken, oyster sauce, rice
wine, sesame oil, ginger, soy sauce, garlic
and chile. Cover and leave in a cool place
for up to 1 hour, or in the refrigerator up to
8 hours (return to room temperature 30
minutes before cooking). Cut 10 (6-inch)
squares of waxed paper. Lay 1 on the work
surface with a point towards you. Put several
pieces of chicken near the point. Add some
mushroom strips and scallions. Fold the
point over the filling, making a firm crease.
Fold the left and right hand corners to the
middle.

Continue to fold the package over, away
from you. Tuck in the last flap to make a
package about 3x2 inches. Repeat with
remaining chicken and waxed paper. Half
fill a wok or deep fryer with oil and heat to
360-375F (185-190C). Fry packages in
batches for about 8 minutes, pushing them
under occasionally and turning over once or
twice. Remove with a slotted spoon. Keep
warm while cooking remaining packages.
Serve unopened.

Serves 5-6.

─BROILED CHICKEN SKEWERS─

6 large chicken thighs, total weight about 2¼ lbs.
2 cloves garlic, finely chopped
⅔ cup coconut milk
2 teaspoons ground coriander
1 teaspoon each ground cumin and ground turmeric
Juice of 1 lime
Leaves from 8 sprigs cilantro, chopped
3 tablespoons light soy sauce
2 tablespoons fish sauce
3 tablespoons light brown sugar
½ teaspoon crushed dried chiles

Using a sharp knife, slit along underside of each chicken thigh and remove bone, scraping flesh from bone.

Cut each boned thigh into 6 pieces. Put in a bowl. In a small bowl, mix together garlic, coconut milk, cilantro, cumin and turmeric. Pour over chicken. Stir to coat then cover and refrigerate for 2-12 hours. To make sauce, in a small serving bowl, mix together remaining ingredients. Set aside.

Soak 8 short wooden or bamboo skewers for 30 minutes. Preheat broiler. Thread chicken, skin side up, on skewers. Put on oiled broiler rack and cook for 4-5 minutes. Turn over and cook for further 2-3 minutes until juices run clear. Serve with sauce.

Makes 4 to 6 servings.

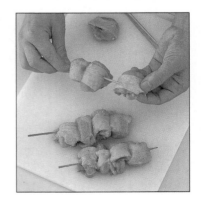

MILD FISH CURRY

3 small onions, chopped
2 cloves garlic, smashed
1 fresh red chile, cored, seeded and chopped
1 (1-inch) piece of ginger root, chopped
2 stalks lemon grass, chopped
2 teaspoons ground turmeric
3 tablespoons peanut oil
2¼ cups coconut milk
1 lb. firm white fish fillet, such as cod, haddock or monkfish, skinned and cubed
3 tablespoons thick coconut milk
2oz. shredded coconut, dry-fried and pounded (see page 8)
Shredded fresh red chile, to garnish

Put onions, garlic, chile, ginger, lemon grass and turmeric in a blender and mix to a paste. Heat oil in a wok or skillet over medium-high heat. Add spice paste and fry for 3-4 minutes until fragrant but not colored.

Stir coconut milk into spice paste. Bring to a boil, stirring, then lower heat and simmer for 3 minutes. Add fish to pan and cook gently for 3-4 minutes until just cooked through. Stir in thick coconut milk and pounded coconut. Serve garnished with shredded chile.

Makes 3 to 4 servings.

──COCONUT CURRIED FISH──

6 cloves garlic, chopped
1 (1-inch) piece of ginger root, chopped
1 large fresh red chile, cored, seeded and chopped
4 tablespoons vegetable oil
1 large onion, quartered and sliced
2 teaspoons ground cumin
½ teaspoon ground turmeric
1¾ cups coconut milk
Salt
1 lb. firm white fish fillet such as cod or halibut, cut
   into 2-inch pieces
Cilantro sprigs and lime wedges, to garnish

Put garlic, ginger and chile in a blender. Add ⅔ cup water. Mix until smooth.

In a wok or sauté pan over medium heat, heat oil. Add onion and fry 5-7 minutes until beginning to color. Add cumin and turmeric and stir for 30 seconds. Stir in garlic mixture. Cook, stirring, for about 2 minutes until liquid has evaporated.

Pour coconut milk into pan. Bring to a boil and boil until sauce is reduced by half. Add salt to taste. Add fish. Spoon sauce over fish so it is covered. Heat to a simmer and cook gently for 4-6 minutes until fish just flakes with tested with point of a sharp knife. Garnish with cilantro sprigs and lime wedges. Serve with rice.

Makes 3 to 4 servings.

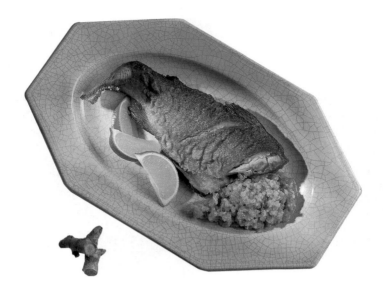

—CRISP FISH WITH TURMERIC—

2 whole fish such as trout or bream, each weighing
about 12 oz.
1 teaspoon ground turmeric
1½ teaspoons salt
½ cup vegetable oil
SAUCE
1 tablespoon tamarind
4 dried red chiles
1 stalk lemon grass, chopped
1 clove garlic, chopped
4 shallots, chopped
1 (¼-inch) piece of galangal, chopped
3 tablespoons vegetable oil
5 oz. peanuts, toasted, skinned and ground
About 2 teaspoons light brown sugar
Salt

To make sauce, soak tamarind in 2 tablespoons hot water for 4 hours. Press firmly
through a sieve. In blender, soak chiles in 2
tablespoons hot water for 10 minutes. Add
lemon grass, garlic, shallots and galangal.
Grind to a paste. In a wok or small skillet
over medium-high heat, heat oil. Add chile
mixture and fry, stirring, for 3 minutes. Add
tamarind liquid, peanuts, and sugar and salt
to taste. Simmer for 2-3 minutes. Set aside.

With point of a sharp knife, score
3 diagonal lines on each side of both fish.
Score each fish lengthways down backbone.
Mix together turmeric and salt. Rub into
fish, working mixture into cuts; wear rubber
gloves if you like. Leave for 1 hour. In a wok
or sauté pan over medium heat, heat oil to
350F (180C). Cook fish for 5-6 minutes per
side until golden and crisp. Remove with
spatula and drain on paper towels. Serve
hot, accompanied by lime wedges and sauce.

Makes 4 servings.

–SPICED FISH IN BANANA LEAVES–

1¼ lbs. white fish fillets
Banana leaves or aluminium foil
Oil for brushing
SPICE PASTE
6 shallots, chopped
2 cloves, garlic, smashed
2 fresh red chiles, cored, seeded and chopped
1 (1-inch) piece of ginger root, chopped
4 candlenuts or cashew nuts
½ teaspoon tamarind paste (see page 10)
2 teaspoons each ground coriander and ground cumin
¼ teaspoon ground turmeric
Salt

For spice paste, put all ingredients in a
blender and mix to a paste.

Cut fish into 4x2-inch pieces ½-inch
thick. Coat top of each piece thickly with
spice paste. If using banana leaves, hold
them over a flame to soften. Oil leaves
thoroughly and cut into pieces to wrap
around pieces of fish (or do this with foil).
Secure with wooden cocktail sticks or
toothpicks.

Preheat grill or broiler. Cook fish packages
for 8-10 minutes, turning halfway through.
Serve with lime wedges, and with banana
leaf or foil partially torn away to reveal fish.

Makes 4 servings.

MARINATED BROILED FISH

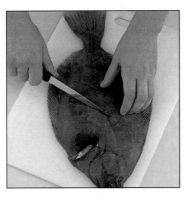

4 flat fish such as flounder or sole, each weighing
   about 12 oz.
4 large cloves garlic, cut into fine slivers
1 (1-inch) piece of ginger root, cut into fine slivers
4 tablespoons peanut oil
4 tablespoons light soy sauce
1 tablespoon sesame oil
1 tablespoon rice wine
4 scallions, thinly sliced

With the point of a sharp knife, cut 5
diagonal slashes, herringbone style, in both
sides of each fish. Place in a shallow dish.

Put garlic, ginger, peanut oil, soy sauce,
sesame oil and rice wine in a small
saucepan. Heat to simmering point and pour
over fish, spooning marinade into slashes.
Refrigerate for at least 1 hour, turning fish
every 30 minutes.

Preheat broiler. Lift fish from marinade and
broil, pale skin side down, for 3 minutes.
Turn carefully and broil for a further 1-2
minutes depending on thickness of fish.
Broil in batches if necessary, keeping broiled
fish warm. Reheat any remaining marinade
and pour over fish. Scatter scallions over
and serve.

Makes 4 servings.

——SPICED SWEET & SOUR FISH——

1 tablespoon cumin seeds
1 teaspoon coriander seeds
3 tablespoons vegetable oil
½ fresh red chile, cored, seeded and chopped
3 cloves garlic, smashed
2 onions, chopped
1-inch shrimp paste, roasted (see page 10)
3½ tablespoons lime juice
3 tablespoons dark soy sauce
Brown sugar
2 whole fish, each weighing about 1½ lbs.

Heat cumin and coriander seeds in skillet over medium-high heat until toasted with a fragrant roasted aroma.

Cool slightly then grind in a small blender, a pestle and mortar or a small bowl using the end of a rolling pin. In a small skillet over medium-high heat, heat oil. Add chile, garlic and onions and fry until lightly browned. Tip into the blender containing the cumin and coriander. Add shrimp paste, lime juice and soy sauce. Mix to a thin paste. Add ½ cup hot water, and sugar to taste. Set aside.

Preheat broiler. Cut 3 deep slashes on both sides of each fish and score along backbone. Cook for 5-6 minutes per side, depending on thickness. The flesh should just flake when tested with point of a sharp knife, and the skin should be brown. Reheat sauce and pour some over each fish. Serve remaining sauce separately.

Makes 4 to 5 servings.

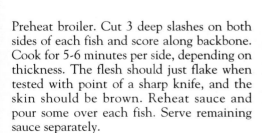

—SARAWAK MARINATED FISH—

1 lb. very fresh white fish fillets, skinned and thinly
  sliced
⅓ cup lime juice
2 fresh red chiles, cored, seeded and chopped
Salt
1 (2-inch) piece of ginger root, grated
6 shallots, finely chopped
2 sprigs cilantro, chopped
2 inner celery stalks, chopped

Put fish in a nonreactive dish. Pour over all
but 2 tablespoons lime juice and leave for at
least 30 minutes, stirring gently occasionally,
until fish turns opaque.

Meanwhile, in a mortar and using a pestle,
pound chiles with a pinch of salt. Mix with
remaining lime juice.

Drain lime juice from fish. Sprinkle ginger,
shallots, cilantro and celery over fish.
Trickle chile mixture evenly over fish and
stir gently to mix ingredients together.
Serve immediately.

Makes 4 servings.

—— FISH STEAKS WITH CHILE ——

5 dried red chiles, cored and seeded
½ small red pepper, chopped
5 shallots, chopped
4 cloves garlic, chopped
4 tablespoons vegetable oil
1 lb. fish steaks such as cod, monkfish, salmon, snapper
Cilantro sprigs, to garnish
Rice and lime juice, to serve

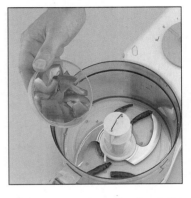

Put chiles in a blender. Add ¼ cup hot water and leave until softened. Add red pepper, shallots and garlic. Mix to a coarse paste.

In a skillet over medium heat, heat 2 tablespoons oil. Add fish and fry until lightly browned on both sides and almost, but not quite, cooked through. Using a spatula, transfer to paper towels to drain.

Add remaining oil to pan. Add chile paste and cook over medium-high heat for about 3 minutes until paste looks dryish. Stir in 2 tablespoons water. Lower heat, return fish to pan and baste with chile paste. Cook gently for 1-2 minutes, basting with paste. Garnish with cilantro, and serve with rice and with plenty of lime juice squeezed over.

Makes 3 to 4 servings.

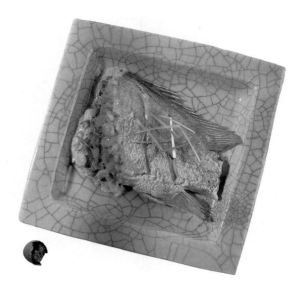

SWEET & SOUR FISH

1 teaspoon tamarind
1 small onion, chopped
3 cloves garlic, crushed
2 fresh red chiles, cored, seeded and chopped
1 (1-inch) piece of ginger root, chopped
1 (1½- lbs) whole fish such as red snapper
4 tablespoons vegetable oil
1¼ cups coconut milk
6 scallions, including some green, sliced
Sugar and salt
Shredded scallions, to garnish

In a small bowl, soak tamarind in 2 table-spoons hot water. Strain through sieve, pressing down firmly. Reserve liquid.

Put onion, garlic, chiles and ginger in a blender. Mix briefly. Cut 4 deep slashes in both sides of fish. In a wok or large skillet over medium-high heat, heat oil. Add fish to pan and and cook for 4-5 minutes per side until flesh just flakes when tested with point of a sharp knife. Transfer to paper towels to drain. Keep warm.

Add ginger mixture to pan and fry for 3-4 minutes until softened but not colored. Stir in tamarind liquid and coconut milk. Add scallions and simmer for 2-3 minutes. Season with sugar and salt to taste. Put fish on a serving plate and pour sauce over. Garnish with scallions.

Makes 2 servings.

—MUSSELS IN HOT SPICY SAUCE—

4 dried red chiles, seeded
2 teaspoons shrimp paste, roasted (see page 10)
1 small onion, chopped
1 (1-inch) piece of fresh galangal
4 cloves garlic, 3 coarsely chopped and 1 finely
  chopped
1 lemon grass stalk, sliced
6-8 candlenuts or cashew nuts
1 teaspoon paprika
4 tablespoons vegetable oil
2-3 lbs. live mussels, cleaned

Put chiles in a small bowl. Add 4 tablespoons hot water and soak until slightly softened. Pour into a blender.

Add shrimp paste, onion, galangal, coarsely chopped garlic, lemon grass, nuts and paprika. Mix to a paste, adding a little extra water if necessary. In a wok or large sauté pan, heat oil over medium-high heat. Add finely chopped garlic and stir until just beginning to brown. Add spice paste and stir for 3 minutes.

Pour in 1½ cups water and bring to a boil. Add all the mussels. Return quickly to boil then cover pan and cook over medium-high heat for 3-5 minutes, shaking and tossing pan halfway through, until all mussels have opened; discard any mussels that remain closed. Serve mussels in deep bowls with cooking juices spooned over.

Makes 2 to 4 servings.

FRAGRANT SHRIMP

2 dried shrimps
2 tablespoons vegetable oil
5 whole small fresh red chiles
1 small onion, finely chopped
3 cloves garlic, finely chopped
1 (1-inch) piece of fresh ginger root, grated
1 teaspoon curry powder
Leaves from 2 stalks of fresh curry leaves
1 lb. raw unpeeled medium shrimp, peeled and
　deveined
1 tablespoon yellow bean sauce
1 teaspoon oyster sauce
1 teaspoon dark soy sauce
2 teaspoons rice wine
Pinch of sugar

Soak dried shrimps in hot water for 10 minutes. Drain and pound in a mortar or mix in a small blender. In a wok or sauté pan, heat oil over medium heat. Add chiles, onion, garlic and ginger. Fry for 1 minute. Add curry powder and curry leaves. Stir for 30 seconds.

Stir in shrimp and dried shrimps then add yellow bean sauce, oyster sauce and soy sauce. Bring to a simmer, cover pan then cook gently for 2-3 minutes until shrimp beginning to turn pink. Add rice wine, and sugar to taste. Increase heat and stir for a few seconds. Serve immediately.

Makes 4 servings.

──SHRIMP ROBED IN SPICES──

8 candlenuts or cashew nuts
2 teaspoons lime juice
2 large shallots, chopped
4 cloves garlic, crushed
1 (1-inch) piece of galangal, chopped
1 (1-inch) piece of ginger root, chopped
1 stalk lemon grass, chopped
½ teaspoon ground turmeric
4 tablespoons vegetable oil
1¼ lbs. raw unpeeled medium shrimp, peeled and
  deveined

Put nuts in a blender and grind to a powder. Transfer to a small bowl. Stir in lime juice and 1 tablespoon water. Set aside.

Put shallots, garlic, galangal, ginger, lemon grass and turmeric in blender. Add 2-3 tablespoons water and mix to a paste. In a wok or large nonstick skillet over medium heat, heat oil. Add spice paste and cook, stirring, for about 5 minutes until reduced and reddish-brown in color.

Add shrimp and nut mixture. Increase heat to high and fry, stirring, for 2-3 minutes until shrimp are cooked and spice mixture clings to them. Using a slotted spoon transfer to a warm plate, leaving all oil behind.

Makes 3 to 4 servings.

SHRIMP KEBABS

½ cup vegetable oil
6 tablespoons lime juice
1 (½-inch) piece of ginger root, grated
2 large cloves garlic, finely crushed
1 fresh red chile, cored, seeded and finely chopped
Leaves from a small bunch of cilantro, chopped
1 tablespoon light soy sauce
½ teaspoon light brown sugar
1½ lbs. raw, unpeeled jumbo shrimp

Soak 8 long wooden or bamboo skewers in water for 20-30 minutes. In a bowl, whisk together oil, lime juice, ginger, garlic and chile. Stir in cilantro, soy sauce and sugar.

Drain skewers. Thread shrimp on skewers. Place them in a shallow nonreactive dish. Pour ginger mixture evenly over shrimp. Turn skewers, cover and refrigerate for 1-2 hours, turning occasionally. Return to room temperature for 15 minutes. Drain skewers and bring marinade to a boil in a small saucepan; reserve.

Preheat broiler. Transfer kebabs to oiled broiler rack; reserve marinade. Cook shrimp 2-3 inches from heat, for 4-6 minutes, turning halfway through cooking time, until they turn pink. Brush with reserved marinade occasionally. Serve accompanied by Dipping Sauce (see page 85).

Makes 4 servings.

──CHICKEN IN SPICED SAUCE──

2 tablespoons vegetable oil
6 each chicken thighs and drumsticks
2 lemon grass stalks, chopped
4 shallots, chopped
4 cloves garlic, chopped
1 (2½-inch) piece of ginger root, chopped
3 tablespoons ground coriander
2 teaspoons ground turmeric
4 fresh bay leaves
1½ cups coconut milk
4 tablespoons Chinese chile sauce
About 2 tablespoons brown sugar, or to taste
½ cup roasted candlenuts or cashew nuts, finely
  chopped
Salt

In a large skillet over medium heat, heat oil.
Add chicken and brown evenly. Transfer to
paper towels to drain. Pour all but 1½
tablespoons fat from pan. Put lemon grass,
shallots, garlic and ginger in a blender. Mix
to a paste. Gently heat pan of fat, add spice
paste and stir for 2 minutes. Stir in
coriander, turmeric and bay leaves for 1
minute. Stir in coconut milk, chile sauce,
sugar, nuts and salt for a further minute.

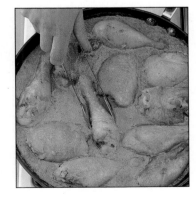

Return chicken to pan and turn in sauce.
Cover and cook gently for 20 minutes,
stirring and turning chicken frequently,
until chicken juices run clear. Discard bay
leaves before serving.

Makes 6 servings.

–BRAISED CHICKEN WITH SPICES–

4 each chicken thighs and drumsticks, total weight about 2¼ lbs.
4 cloves garlic, chopped
2 shallots, chopped
1 (2-inch) piece of ginger root, chopped
1¾ cups coconut milk
2 teaspoons each ground coriander and ground cumin
¼ teaspoon ground turmeric
2 tablespoons vegetable oil
6 green cardamom pods
6 each star anise and dried red chiles
1 cinnamon stick
4 whole cloves
20 fresh curry leaves

Skin chicken pieces and set aside.

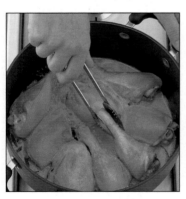

Put garlic, shallots, ginger, coconut milk, coriander, cumin and turmeric into a small blender. Mix to a fine paste. In a heavy-bottom saucepan large enough to hold chicken in a single layer, heat oil over medium heat. Add cardamom pods, star anise, chiles, cinnamon, cloves and curry leaves. Fry, stirring, for 2-3 minutes. Add ⅓ of the coconut milk mixture. Bring to boil and add chicken. Turn to coat and cook for 5 minutes.

Add remaining coconut milk mixture. Bring to a simmer, lower heat and cook gently, uncovered, for 50 minutes, stirring frequently. Cook for a further 10 minutes, stirring every minute. The chicken should be golden brown and most of the milk evaporated. Pour away oily residue. Increase heat to high. Add 3-4 tablespoons water and stir to deglaze pan. Serve chicken with Thai rice and sauce.

Makes 4 servings.

—CHICKEN & PINEAPPLE CURRY—

5 shallots, chopped
3 large fresh red chiles, cored, seeded and chopped
3 cloves garlic, crushed
1 (2-inch) piece of galangal, chopped
1 stalk lemon grass, chopped
2 tablespoons vegetable oil
1½ lbs. boneless, skinless chicken breasts, cut into
    strips
2 tablespoons light brown sugar
1¾ cups coconut milk
2 teaspoons tamarind paste (see page 10)
2 tablespoons fish sauce
4 kaffir lime leaves
1 small pineapple, about 1 lb., thinly sliced
Grated rind and juice of 1 lime, or to taste
Small handful cilantro leaves, chopped

Put shallots, chiles, garlic, galangal and lemon grass in a small blender. Mix to a paste; add 1 tablespoon of the oil, if necessary. In a wok or sauté pan, heat remaining oil. Add chicken and stir-fry until just turning pale golden brown. Remove and set aside.

Stir chile paste into pan and stir-fry for 3-4 minutes until fragrant. Stir in sugar, coconut milk, tamarind, fish sauce and kaffir lime leaves. Bring to a boil, and boil for 4-5 minutes until reduced by half and lightly thickened. Return chicken to pan. Add pineapple and simmer for 3-4 minutes until chicken juices run clear. Add the lime rind, and lime juice to taste. Stir in cilantro.

Makes 6 servings.

DEVIL'S CURRY

6 tablespoons vegetable oil
6 shallots, thinly sliced
3 cloves garlic, thinly sliced
1 teaspoon black mustard seeds, lightly crushed
3½ lbs. chicken, cut up, or small chicken portions
10oz. small potatoes, halved
2 teaspoons mustard powder
2 tablespoons rice vinegar
1 tablespoon dark soy sauce
SPICE PASTE
10 fresh red chiles, cored, seeded and chopped
1 (2-inch) piece of ginger root, chopped
6 shallots, chopped
3 cloves garlic, chopped
1 tablespoon ground coriander
½ teaspoon ground turmeric
8 candlenuts or cashew nuts

To make spice paste, put all ingredients in a blender and mix to a paste. In a large wok or sauté pan, heat oil over medium-high heat. Add shallots and garlic and fry until lightly browned. Stir in spice paste and cook for about 5 minutes, stirring. Add mustard seeds, stir once or twice then add chicken. Cook, stirring frequently, until chicken pieces turn white.

Add potatoes and 2½ cups water. Bring to a boil, cover and simmer for 15 minutes. Stir together mustard, vinegar and soy sauce. Stir into pan, re-cover and cook for another 15-20 minutes until chicken is tender, stirring occasionally.

Makes 4 to 6 servings.

———AROMATIC CHICKEN———

2 teaspoons tamarind paste (see page 10)
Salt
1 (3½-lb). chicken, cut into 10 pieces, or chicken
  portions, chopped
12 fresh green chiles, cored, seeded and chopped
2 small onions, chopped
5 cloves garlic, smashed
1 ripe tomato, chopped
5 tablespoons vegetable oil
4 kaffir lime leaves
1 stalk lemon grass, crushed

Blend tamarind with 1 teaspoon salt and
2 tablespoons hot water. Pour mixture over
chicken and rub in. Leave for 1 hour.

Put chiles, onions, garlic and tomato in a
blender. Mix to a paste. In a wok or large
heavy sauté pan, heat oil. Add chicken and
marinade. Turn to brown on both sides then
remove with a slotted spoon.

Add spice paste, lime leaves and lemon grass
to pan. Cook, stirring, for 6-7 minutes until
paste is browned. Return chicken to pan,
add 1¼ cups water and bring to a simmer.
Cover and simmer gently for 30 minutes
until chicken juices run clear, turning
chicken occasionally.

Makes 4 servings.

MALAY CHICKEN

8 boneless chicken thighs, total weight about 1½ lbs.
1 bunch of scallions, white part finely chopped
2 tablespoons chopped fresh cilantro
2 oz. creamed coconut, chopped
1 clove garlic, crushed and finely chopped
½ fresh red chile, cored, seeded and chopped
2 teaspoons sunflower oil
1 teaspoon sesame oil
2 tablespoons lime juice
2 teaspoons each ground roasted cumin seeds and
   coriander seeds
Salt
Lime slices
Cilantro sprigs, to garnish

Open out the chicken thighs. Mix together the scallions and cilantro and spoon an equal quantity on each opened chicken thigh. Reform the thighs. Put in a single layer in a nonreactive dish. Put coconut in a bowl and stir in scant 1 cup boiling water until dissolved. Stir in garlic, chile, oils, lime juice, spices and salt. Pour over chicken, turn to coat in marinade, cover and refrigerate overnight.

Preheat broiler or grill. Transfer chicken to room temperature. Soak bamboo skewers in water for 20-30 minutes. Remove chicken from marinade (reserve marinade) and thread 1 or 2 chicken thighs onto each skewer with a lime slice. Grill or broil for about 20 minutes, basting with remaining marinade, until chicken juices run clear when tested with the point of a sharp knife. Garnish with cilantro sprigs.

Makes 4 servings.

──────NONYA CHICKEN──────

2 tablespoons vegetable oil
1¾ lbs. chicken portions, cut into large bite-size
  pieces
2 fresh red chiles, sliced into rings
1 tablespoon dark soy sauce
1 tablespoon light soy sauce
1½ teaspoons light brown sugar
1 onion, sliced into (¼-inch) rings
Sesame oil for sprinkling
Toasted sesame seeds, to garnish

In a wok or large skillet over medium-high heat, heat oil. Add chicken and fry until evenly browned.

Using a slotted spoon transfer to paper towels to drain. Add chiles to pan and stir-fry for 30 seconds. Return chicken to pan. Add soy sauces, sugar and 4 tablespoons water. Bring to a simmer. Stir, cover pan and cook gently for 10 minutes, stirring occasionally.

Stir in onion, re-cover pan and continue to cook gently. stirring occasionally, for 5 minutes or until chicken juices run clear when pierced with a sharp knife and onion is soft. Sprinkle in a few drops of sesame oil. Serve scattered with toasted sesame seeds to garnish.

Makes 3 to 4 servings.

SPICED CHICKEN

8 chicken thighs, boned (see page 29) and chopped
3 tablespoons vegetable oil
1 clove garlic, finely chopped
2 tablespoons fish sauce
6 shallots, finely chopped
Cilantro leaves, to garnish
MARINADE
2 small fresh red chiles, cored, seeded and chopped
1 stalk lemon grass, chopped
1 clove garlic, crushed
1 (1½-inch) piece of ginger root, chopped
1 tablespoon ground turmeric
1 (8-oz.) canned tomatoes
1 tablespoon light brown sugar
Salt

To make marinade, put all ingredients in a blender and mix together well. Put chicken in a nonreactive bowl. Pour marinade over chicken. Stir together, cover and refrigerate overnight. Return bowl of chicken to room temperature for 30 minutes. In a wok or heavy sauté pan over high heat, heat oil. Add garlic and fry for 30 seconds. Add chicken and marinade. Stir and toss together, then stir in fish sauce and 4 tablespoons hot water. Cover, lower heat and simmer for 5 minutes.

Add shallots and continue to cook, uncovered, stirring occasionally, for about 10 minutes until chicken juices run clear. Serve garnished with cilantro.

Makes 4 servings.

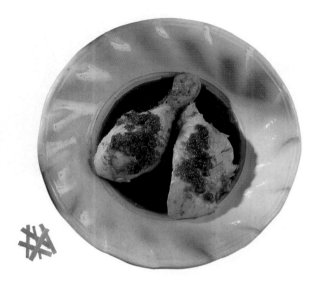

GINGER & SOY ROAST CHICKEN

1 (1½-inch) piece of ginger root, coarsely chopped
1 onion, coarsely chopped
3 cloves garlic, coarsely chopped
1 (3½-lb.) chicken
5 tablespoons vegetable oil
3 tablespoons dark soy sauce
3 tablespoons rice vinegar
2½ tablespoons light brown sugar

Put ginger, onion and garlic in a blender. Mix to a paste, adding just enough water so the blender blades work.

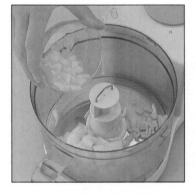

Put chicken in a roasting pan. Rub inside and outside of chicken with half of ginger mixture. Cover and leave for 30 minutes. Put remaining ginger paste in a bowl and stir in oil, soy sauce, rice vinegar, sugar and 6 tablespoons water.

Preheat oven to 350F(180C). Prop up tail end of chicken. Pour as much soy sauce mixture as possible into cavity of chicken. Roast chicken for 25 minutes, basting occasionally with remaining soy mixture. Pour remaining soy mixture around chicken and cook for a further 50 minutes, basting occasionally, until chicken juices run clear. Stir a little water into pan if sauce begins to dry out too much.

Makes 4 servings.

CHICKEN WITH RICE

1 (1-inch) piece of ginger root, grated
4 scallions, including some green, finely chopped
2 teaspoons rice wine
1 (2½-lb.) chicken
4 cloves garlic, lightly crushed
1¼ cups long grain rice
TO SERVE
1 (2-inch) piece of ginger root, grated
¾ teaspoon salt
2 teaspoons each soy sauce and rice vinegar
1 teaspoon sesame oil
2 scallions, including some green, sliced

In a small bowl, mix together ginger, scallions and rice wine. Rub over chicken and put some in cavity. Set aside for 30 minutes. Put chicken in a large saucepan; cover with water. Add garlic and bring to a boil over medium heat. Skim off any impurities. Cover pan and poach for 25 minutes. Refrigerate in broth for 1½ hours. Remove chicken and plunge into a bowl of water and ice cubes for 10 minutes. Strain stock and measure 2 cups. Remove chicken skin and cut meat into chunks. Keep warm.

In a small serving bowl, mix ginger and salt. In another bowl, mix soy sauce, rice vinegar and sesame oil. In a third bowl, put scallions. Bring measured stock to a boil; add rice. Return to a boil, stir, cover and simmer for 12 minutes. Remove from heat and leave for 5 minutes until tender. Divide rice among 4 warm serving bowls and put chicken on top. Bring remaining stock to a boil. Spoon over chicken or serve separately. Serve with accompaniments.

Makes 4 servings.

──────PORK WITH TAMARIND──────

4 dried red chiles, cored and seeded
1 large onion, chopped
4 candlenuts or cashew nuts
2 tablespoons vegetable oil
1½ lbs. pork shoulder, cut into large bite-size pieces
2 tablespoons tamarind paste (see page 10)
2 tablespoons dark soy sauce
1 tablespoon yellow bean sauce
1 tablespoon light brown sugar
Sliced fresh chiles, to garnish (optional)

Put dried chiles in a blender. Add 4 tablespoons hot water and leave until slightly softened. Add onion and nuts; mix to a smooth paste.

In a sauté pan, preferably nonstick, heat oil over medium-high heat. Add meat in batches and fry until an even light brown. Using a slotted spoon transfer to paper towels to drain.

Add chile paste to pan and fry for about 5 minutes. Stir in pork, tamarind paste, soy sauce, yellow bean sauce, sugar and 1½ cups water. Bring to a simmer, cover pan then cook gently for 30-40 minutes, stirring occasionally, until pork is very tender. Serve garnished with sliced fresh chiles, if liked.

Makes 4 servings.

MIXED SATAY

12 oz. pork fillet, chilled, thinly sliced
12 oz. beef steak, chilled, thinly sliced
½ lime
2 teaspoons each ground coriander and ground cumin
1 teaspoon ground turmeric
1 tablespoon light brown sugar
4 tablespoons coconut milk
12 large raw shrimps (jumbo shrimp), peeled, tails left on, deveined
Oil for brushing
Satay Sauce (see opposite)

Lay each pork slice between sheets of plastic wrap and beat with a rolling pin until fairly thin. Cut slices into 1-inch wide strips.

Cut beef into strips about same size as pork. Put meats into a nonreactive bowl. Squeeze lime juice over. In a small bowl, mix together coriander, cumin, turmeric, sugar and coconut milk to make a fairly dry paste. Add shrimp to dish with meat and spoon coconut mixture over to coat thoroughly. Cover and marinate for 30 minutes, or overnight in the refrigerator.

Heat grill or broiler. Soak bamboo skewers in water for 20-30 minutes. Thread pork strips, beef strips and shrimp onto separate skewers. Brush with oil and cook at a very high heat for 10 minutes, turning frequently. Shrimp should have turned opaque with bright pink tails, pork should be cooked through and beef still be pink in center. Meanwhile, heat satay sauce. Serve sauce with skewers.

Makes 6 servings.

SATAY SAUCE

3oz. roasted peanuts
1 fresh red chile, cored, seeded and chopped
1 clove garlic, chopped
4 tablespoons red curry paste
Scant 1¾ cups coconut milk
Squeeze of lime juice
2 tablespoons light brown sugar

Put peanuts, chile and garlic in a blender. Mix together, then add curry paste, 2 tablespoons of the coconut milk and a squeeze of lime juice. Mix to blend evenly.

Pour mixture into a saucepan. Stir in remaining coconut milk and the sugar. Bring to a boil, stirring, then boil for 2 minutes.

Lower heat and simmer for 10 minutes, stirring occasionally. Add a little water if sauce becomes too thick.

Makes 6 servings.

BEEF IN CHILE SAUCE

8 dried red chiles, cored, seeded and chopped
2 small onions, chopped
1 (2-inch) piece of ginger root, chopped
1½lbs. lean beef, cut into bite-size pieces
1 tablespoon each ground coriander and cumin
1 tablespoon tomato ketchup
2 teaspoons each turmeric and paprika
2 tablespoons vegetable oil
2 cloves garlic, crushed
1 (1-inch) cinnamon stick
Seeds from 3 cardamom pods, crushed
½ star anise
Sugar and salt
1 onion, sliced into thick rings

Put chiles in a small blender. Add 4 tablespoons hot water and leave until slightly softened. Add half of small onions and half of ginger to blender and mix to a paste. Put beef in a large bowl. Add spice paste from blender, coriander, cumin, tomato ketchup, turmeric and paprika. Stir together. Cover and refrigerate for at least 1 hour to marinate.

In a wok, heat oil over medium-high heat. Add remaining onion and ginger, and the garlic. Fry, stirring, for 3 minutes until lightly browned. Stir in next 3 ingredients for 1 minute. Add beef and marinade and cook over medium-high heat, stirring, for 5 minutes. Add 1½ cups water, and sugar and salt to taste. Cover pan. Simmer very gently for 1¼ hours or until beef is tender. Stir occasionally. Add onion rings and cook for 3-5 minutes or until soft.

Makes 4 to 6 servings.

—"DRY" BEEF WITH COCONUT—

4 tablespoons vegetable oil
6 shallots, finely chopped
3 cloves garlic, finely chopped
1 fresh red chile, cored, seeded and finely chopped
1½ lbs. lean beef, thinly sliced and cut into ½-inch
   strips
1 tablespoon light brown sugar
1½ teaspoons ground cumin
1 teaspoon ground coriander
Squeeze of lime juice
Salt
½ fresh coconut, grated, or 2⅔ cups shredded
   coconut

In a wok or sauté pan, heat 1 tablespoon oil over medium heat. Add shallots, garlic and chile and fry for about 5 minutes, stirring occasionally, until softened but not browned. Add beef, sugar, cumin, coriander, lime juice, salt to taste and ⅔ cup water. Cover pan tightly and simmer gently for 30 minutes, stirring occasionally.

Uncover pan, stir in coconut until all the liquid has been absorbed. Stir in the remaining oil and continue stirring until the coconut begins to brown.

Makes 6 servings.

CURRIED COCONUT BEEF

6⅔ cups coconut milk
4 fresh bay leaves
1 (3-lb.) beef round steak, cut into (2-inch) cubes
CURRY PASTE
6 shallots, chopped
6 cloves garlic, smashed
6 fresh red chiles, cored, seeded and chopped
1 (3-inch) piece galangal, chopped
2 stalks lemon grass, chopped
1 (1-inch) stick cinnamon
12 whole cloves
1 teaspoon ground turmeric

Mix all curry paste ingredients in a blender. Add a little coconut milk, if necessary.

In a saucepan, combine curry paste and coconut milk. Add bay leaves and bring to a boil over high heat, stirring occasionally. Lower heat to medium and cook sauce, stirring occasionally, for 15 minutes.

Stir in beef. Simmer, uncovered, stirring occasionally, for 2 hours. Reduce heat to very low and cook beef for a further 1½-2 hours until sauce is quite thick. Stir frequently to prevent sticking. Skim fat and oil from surface. Serve with boiled rice.

Makes 8 servings.

LAMB CURRY

2 onions, chopped
3 cloves garlic, smashed
4 fresh red chiles, cored, seeded and chopped
1 stalk lemon grass, chopped
1½ tablespoons chopped ginger root
2 teaspoons ground coriander
1 teaspoon ground cumin
3½ cups coconut milk
2¼ lbs. lamb, cut into (2-inch) cubes
Juice of 1 lime
1½ teaspoons light brown sugar
Salt

Put onions, garlic, chiles, lemon grass, ginger, coriander and cumin in a blender. Add about ⅔ cup of the coconut milk and mix together well. Pour into a large saucepan. Stir in 1¼ cups coconut milk and 3 cups + 2 tablespoons water and bring to a simmer. Add lamb and lime juice. Simmer gently, uncovered, stirring occasionally, for about 2 hours until meat is tender and liquid has evaporated.

Add a little boiling water if liquid evaporates too quickly. Stir in remaining coconut milk and the sugar. Add salt to taste and simmer for about 5 minutes. Serve with boiled rice.

Makes 4 to 6 servings.

──SINGAPORE STEAMBOAT──

6 oz. fillet of beef, well chilled
6 oz. pork tenderloin, well chilled
6 oz. lamb fillet, well chilled
6 oz. boneless, skinless chicken breast, well chilled
12 oz. thin rice noodles
4 oz. each snow peas, green beans, baby corn, oyster
  mushrooms, shiitake mushrooms, asparagus spears,
  cut into bite-size pieces

Thinly slice beef, pork, lamb and chicken.
Cover with plastic wrap and set aside. Cook
noodles according to package instructions.
Drain, refresh under running cold water.
Drain again, cover and set aside.

SHRIMP BALLS
12 oz. raw, peeled shrimp
1½-2½ teaspoons cornstarch
2 small scallions, finely chopped
1 small egg white, lightly beaten

Put shrimp and 1½ teaspoons cornstarch
into blender and mix until smooth. Mix in
scallion. Stir in egg white and more
cornstarch if necessary to bind mixture,
which should be firm enough to handle.
With wet hands, roll mixture into walnut-
size balls. Refrigerate until required.

CHILE VINEGAR
3 tablespoons rice vinegar
1½ tablespoons water
2 teaspoons sugar
½-1 fresh red chile, cored, seeded and finely sliced

In a bowl, mix all the ingredients together.

DIPPING SAUCE
2 tablespoons tomato paste
2 tablespoons water
1 teaspoon soy sauce
1 teaspoon toasted sesame oil
1 fresh red chile, cored, seeded and finely chopped

In a bowl, mix all the ingredients together.

COCONUT SAUCE
2 teaspoons peanut oil
1 small onion, finely chopped
1 (2-inch) lemon grass stalk, bruised and thinly
  sliced
¾ teaspoon crushed coriander seeds
3 oz. piece of coconut cream
About 3 tablespoons stock (see below)

In a skillet or saucepan, heat oil. Add
onion, lemon grass and coriander seeds and
fry until the onion has softened. Stir in
coconut cream until melted. Add enough
stock to make a dipping sauce.

STOCK
4¼ cups chicken or vegetable stock
1½ tablespoons chopped cilantro
2 inches thick end of lemon grass stalk, thinly sliced
2 scallions, thinly sliced

In a saucepan, bring stock ingredients to the
boil, then pour into a warm fondue pot or
heavy flameproof casserole set over a
burner. To serve, dip the meat, shrimp balls
and vegetables into the stock to cook, then
transfer them to plates to eat with the
sauces and chile vinegar.

When all the meat, fish and vegetables have
been eaten, either warm the noodles in the
hotpot, or dunk them in a bowl or saucepan
of boiling water, then drain and divide them
among bowls. Ladle remaining stock, which
will have become concentrated, into the
bowls.

Makes 6 servings.

To serve: Use fondue forks, chopsticks,
Chinese wire mesh baskets or long wooden
skewers.

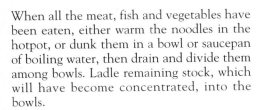

FRIED RICE NOODLES

8oz. dried rice stick noodles, ½-inch wide
2 tablespoons vegetable oil
3 small onions, sliced into thin rings
2 cloves garlic, finely chopped
3 fresh red chiles, seeded, cored and finely chopped
3 Chinese pork sausages, total weight about 6oz.,
  thinly sliced diagonally
8oz. raw unpeeled tiger shrimps, peeled and
  deveined
2 eggs, beaten
4oz. bean sprouts
3 tablespoons light soy sauce
4 tablespoons chicken stock
2 scallions, including some green, cut diagonally into
  (¼-inch) pieces

In a bowl, soak rice stick noodles in hot water for 30 minutes or until softened. Drain well. In a wok or sauté pan, heat oil over medium-high heat. Add onions and stir-fry for 3-4 minutes or until starting to brown. Add garlic, chiles and Chinese sausage and stir-fry for about 30 seconds until fragrant. Add shrimps and stir-fry for 1-1½ minutes until they just turn pink.

Increase heat to high. Quickly stir in eggs, then add bean sprouts, rice sticks, soy sauce and stock. Stir for about 1 minute. Serve sprinkled with the scallions.

Makes 4 servings.

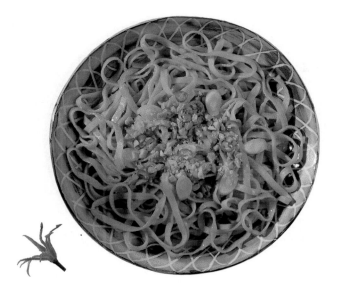

–NOODLES WITH PEANUT SAUCE–

8oz. fresh thin Chinese egg noodles
2 tablespoons sesame oil
1oz. plus 1 tablespoon unsalted roast peanuts
1 clove garlic, crushed
1 tablespoon light soy sauce
2 teaspoons Chinese black vinegar
1 teaspoon light brown sugar
1 tablespoon peanut oil
Few drops hot chile oil
White part of scallion, thinly sliced and fresh red
   chile, very thinly sliced, to garnish

Bring a large saucepan of water to a boil.
Add noodles, return to boil, stir, cover pan
and boil until just tender.

Drain well and turn into a serving bowl.
Toss with 1 tablespoon sesame oil. Set aside.
In a blender or a spice grinder, crush the 1
tablespoon peanuts. Set aside. Put
remaining peanuts and sesame oil, garlic,
soy sauce, vinegar, sugar and peanut oil in a
blender. Add ¼ cup water. Mix to a smooth
sauce. Add chile oil to taste.

To serve, pour peanut sauce over noodles.
Toss to mix. Sprinkle the crushed peanuts
on top, and garnish with scallion and chile
slices.

Makes 3 or 4 side-dish servings.

-NOODLES WITH BEAN SPROUTS-

8 oz. fresh thin Chinese egg noodles
2 tablespoons sesame oil
1 clove garlic, finely crushed
3 tablespoons light soy sauce
1 tablespoon rice vinegar
½ teaspoon light brown sugar
½ fresh red chile, cored, seeded and very finely
  chopped
4 oz. bean sprouts
4 crisp inner Romaine lettuce leaves, shredded

Bring a large saucepan of water to a boil.
Add noodles, return to boil, stir, cover and
boil according to instructions on package,
until just tender.

Drain well and turn into a warm serving
bowl. Toss with 1 tablespoon sesame oil. Set
aside. Put remaining sesame oil, garlic, soy
sauce, vinegar, sugar and chile in a blender.
Mix together.

Scatter bean sprouts and lettuce shreds over
noodles. Stir sesame oil dressing and pour
over noodles and vegetables. Transfer to
serving dish, toss and serve.

Makes 3 or 4 side-dish servings.

—CHICKEN & SHRIMP NOODLES—

8oz. boneless, skinless chicken breast, very thinly
  sliced
8oz. raw shrimp, peeled and deveined
5 tablespoons peanut oil
1 tablespoon sesame oil
1 teaspoon ground coriander
Pinch of Chinese five-spice powder
4oz. thin dried Chinese egg noodles
2oz. each snow peas and green beans, halved
2 cloves garlic, finely crushed
1½ teaspoons grated ginger root
2 fresh red chiles, cored, seeded and finely chopped
1 tablespoon dark soy sauce
1 tablespoon lime juice
2 tablespoons chopped fresh cilantro
Toasted candlenuts or cashew nuts

Put chicken and shrimp into a nonreactive
bowl. Stir together 1 table-spoon peanut oil,
1 teaspoon sesame oil, ground coriander and
five-spice powder. Pour over chicken and
shrimp. Stir until evenly coated. Cook
noodles according to package instructions.
Meanwhile, in a wok or sauté pan, heat
2 tablespoons peanut oil. Add chicken and
shrimp and stir-fry for 2 minutes. Using a
slotted spoon, transfer to paper towels to
drain. Add vegetables to pan and stir-fry for
1 minute.

Transfer chicken and shrimp to serving
bowl. Keep warm. In a small pan, heat
remaining peanut oil and sesame oil. Add
garlic, ginger and chiles and fry gently for 4-
5 minutes until softened but not colored.
Whisk in soy sauce, lime juice and 2
tablespoons water. Bring to a boil then
remove from heat. Drain noodles and
quickly toss with chicken and garlic
mixtures. Serve warm or cold sprinkled with
chopped cilantro and toasted nuts.

Makes 4 servings.

NOODLES WITH FISH

3 tablespoons tamarind
8 oz. rice stick noodles
12 oz. mixed white fish and snapper, salmon or trout
fillets
4 fresh red chiles, cored, seeded and finely chopped
1 lemon grass stalk, crushed, thinly sliced
8 scallions, thinly sliced
1½ teaspoons shrimp paste, roasted (see page 10)
6 oz. peeled raw medium shrimp
8 oz. dried medium Chinese egg noodles
1 tablespoon light brown sugar
¾ teaspoon ground turmeric
6 shallots, very thinly sliced
Leaves from small bunch of mixed basil and mint

Soak tamarind in 3 tablespoons boiling water for 3 hours. Strain through cheesecloth and set aside. Soak rice sticks in boiling water until softened. Put fish, chiles, lemon grass, scallions and shrimp paste in a saucepan. Add 7 cups water. Bring to a boil. Add shrimp and poach until fish just flakes and shrimp turn pink. Remove fish and shrimp and keep warm.

Bring fish stock to a boil then simmer for 5 minutes. Add egg noodles. Stir then boil, uncovered, until just tender. Cut fish into bite-size pieces. Drain both types of noodle. Add sugar and turmeric to stock, and return to a simmer. Divide noodles among 6 warm bowls. Top with fish, shrimp and shallots. Strain over enough stock to moisten well. Add mint and basil leaves. Serve tamarind juice separately, or sprinkle over noodles before serving.

Makes 6 servings.

—FRIED NOODLES WITH CRAB—

4-6 Chinese mushrooms
12oz. dried Chinese egg noodles
3 tablespoons vegetable oil
1 small onion, finely chopped
3 cloves garlic, finely chopped
1 (¾-inch) piece of fresh ginger root, grated
4oz. boneless, skinless chicken breast, cut into strips
4oz. raw peeled medium shrimp
4oz. choi sum, torn into shreds
Oyster sauce
4oz. cooked crabmeat
Egg strips made from 1 egg (see page 69) and 1
    scallion, including some green, sliced, to garnish

Soak mushrooms in hot water for 15
minutes. Strain, reserving liquid. Slice caps
and discard stalks. Set aside. Cook noodles
in a large saucepan of boiling water
according to package instructions. Drain,
rinse and drain again. Set aside. In a wok or
large skillet, heat oil over medium heat.
Add onion, garlic and ginger and cook for
about 4 minutes until softened but not
brown. Increase heat to high. Add chicken
and stir-fry for 2-3 minutes until opaque.
Add shrimp and stir-fry for 1-1½ minutes
until just turning pink.

Quickly stir in the choi sum, then add the
noodles and mushrooms, plus enough of the
soaking liquid to prevent the dish being dry.
Add oyster sauce to taste. Transfer noodle
mixture to a deep, warm plate. Top with
crab and garnish with egg strips and
scallion.

Makes 3 to 4 servings.

RICE WITH LEMON GRASS

2¼ cups coconut milk
2 stalks lemon grass, bruised
1¼ cups long grain rice, rinsed
Salt

Rinse a heavy saucepan with water. Pour in the coconut milk, add the lemon grass and bring to a boil. Stir in the rice and return to a boil.

Stir rice; add salt to taste. Cover pan and cook very gently for 12 minutes until rice is tender and liquid has been absorbed. Without lifting lid, remove pan from the heat and leave to stand for 30 minutes.

Discard lemon grass. Stir rice with chopsticks or a fork to fluff up grains.

Makes 3 or 4 side-dish servings.

——MALAYSIAN FRIED RICE——

1¼ cups long grain white rice, rinsed
3 tablespoons vegetable oil
2 eggs, beaten
1 onion, chopped
2 fresh red chiles, cored, seeded and chopped
2 cloves garlic, crushed
1 teaspoon shrimp paste
6oz. boneless, skinless chicken breast, cut into thin
  strips
4oz. raw, unpeeled jumbo shrimp, peeled and
  deveined
2 tablespoons dark soy sauce
1 tablespoon light brown sugar
2 scallions, including some green, sliced diagonally

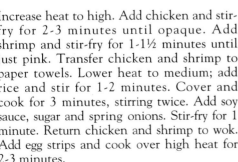

Bring rice to a boil in 2¼ cups water. Stir, cover pan and simmer over low heat for 12 minutes until rice is tender and water is absorbed. Without lifting lid, remove pan from heat and leave for 15 minutes. Uncover and stir. Spread on an oiled tray and leave for 30-60 minutes. Heat 1 tablespoon oil in a wok. Add eggs to make an omelet. When cool, roll up and slice. Mix onions, chiles, garlic and shrimp paste to a paste in a blender. Heat remaining oil in wok over medium-high heat. Add paste and cook for 30 seconds.

Increase heat to high. Add chicken and stir-fry for 2-3 minutes until opaque. Add shrimp and stir-fry for 1-1½ minutes until just pink. Transfer chicken and shrimp to paper towels. Lower heat to medium; add rice and stir for 1-2 minutes. Cover and cook for 3 minutes, stirring twice. Add soy sauce, sugar and spring onions. Stir-fry for 1 minute. Return chicken and shrimp to wok. Add egg strips and cook over high heat for 2-3 minutes.

Makes 4 servings.

SPICED RICE

1 (2-inch) stick cinnamon
1 tablespoon coriander seeds, lightly crushed
Seeds from 1 green cardamom pod, lightly crushed
2 whole star anise
1 small onion, chopped
2 garlic cloves, chopped
1 (¾-inch) piece of ginger root, chopped
1 tablespoon vegetable oil
1¼ cups long grain rice, rinsed
1 teaspoon dark soy sauce
1 tablespoon candlenuts nuts or cashew nuts
2 tablespoons raisins

Put cinnamon, coriander and cardamom seeds and star anise in a saucepan.

Add 3¾ cups water. Simmer uncovered until reduced to 2 cups. Set aside to cool. Put onion, garlic and ginger in a blender and mix to a paste, adding a little of spiced water if necessary. In a saucepan, heat oil over medium-high heat. Add paste and fry for 3-4 minutes, stirring occasionally.

Stir in rice. Strain in spiced water, add soy sauce and bring to a boil. Stir, cover and simmer for about 12 minutes until rice is tender and liquid has been absorbed. Add nuts and raisins and fluff up rice with chopsticks or a fork.

Makes 4 side-dish servings.

SPICED GRILLED SQUASH

2 small butternut squash, quartered and seeded
2 cloves garlic, finely chopped
2 teaspoon ground cumin
2-3 tablespoons vegetable oil
½ lime
Salt and freshly ground black pepper

Using a small, sharp knife make shallow crisscross cuts in the flesh of each squash quarter.

In a bowl, mix together garlic, cumin, oil, a good squeeze of lime juice, and salt and pepper to taste. Brush over flesh side of each piece of squash, working it well into the cuts.

Preheat grill or broiler. Cook squash quarters for 10-15 minutes until lightly browned and flesh is tender. Brush occasionally with any remaining cumin mixture.

Makes 4 side-dish servings.

—STIR-FRIED SUGAR SNAP PEAS—

8oz. sugar snap peas
1½ tablespoons vegetable oil
6 cloves garlic with skins on, lightly bruised
4oz. raw peeled medium shrimp
2 tablespoons light soy sauce
1½ tablespoons oyster sauce
1 teaspoon rice wine
½ cup fish stock or water blended with 1 teaspoon
　cornstarch
Freshly ground black pepper (optional)

Bring a large saucepan of water to a boil.
Quickly add sugar snap peas and
immediately return to a boil. Boil for
5 seconds, then drain thoroughly.

Heat oil in a wok or large skillet over high
heat. Add garlic and stir-fry for a few
seconds. Add shrimp and stir-fry until pink.
Add peas, soy sauce, oyster sauce and rice
wine. Stir-fry for 30 seconds.

Stir in cornstarch mixture and bring to a
boil, stirring. Add black pepper, if liked, and
serve.

Makes 4 servings.

──SPINACH WITH SESAME──

1½ tablespoons oyster sauce
1lb. young spinach leaves
1½ tablespoons vegetable oil
2 cloves garlic, thinly sliced
1 teaspoon sesame oil
Toasted sesame seeds, to garnish

Mix oyster sauce with 1 tablespoon boiling water. Set aside. Bring a large saucepan of water to a boil. Quickly add spinach and return to a boil for 30 seconds. Drain very well.

Transfer spinach to a warm serving dish. Trickle oyster sauce mixture over spinach. Keep warm.

Meanwhile, in a wok or small skillet heat vegetable oil. Add garlic and fry until just turning golden. Scatter over spinach and trickle a little sesame oil over. Scatter sesame seeds on top and serve.

Makes 4 side-dish servings.

OKRA IN SPICE SAUCE

2 tablespoons dried shrimps
3 fresh red chiles, cored, seeded and chopped
4 cloves garlic, chopped
1½ teaspoons shrimp paste
3 shallots, chopped
3 tablespoons vegetable oil
8oz. fresh okra, trimmed
1 tablespoon lime juice
Freshly ground black pepper

Soak dried shrimps in hot water for 10 minutes. Drain and put in a blender. Add chiles, garlic, shrimp paste and shallots. Mix to a paste, adding a little water if necessary.

In a wok or skillet, heat oil over medium-high heat. Add okra and stir for about 5 minutes. Remove with a slotted spoon and set aside.

Add spice paste to pan and stir for 1 minute. Lower heat and return okra to pan with the lime juice, 4 tablespoons water and plenty of black pepper. Bring to a simmer then cook gently, stirring occasionally, for 5 minutes or until okra is tender.

Makes 3 or 4 side-dish servings.

—GREEN BEANS IN SPICED SAUCE—

2 cloves garlic, chopped
1 stalk lemon grass, chopped
6 shallots, chopped
3 tablespoons vegetable oil
2 strips lime rind
2 fresh red chiles, cored, seeded and finely chopped
2 scallions, thickly sliced diagonally
1½lbs. green beans, cut into 1½-inch lengths
1 cup coconut milk
Salt

Put garlic, lemon grass and shallots in a blender. Add 2 tablespoons water and mix to a paste.

In a large skillet, heat oil over medium-high heat. Add spice paste from blender and fry, stirring, for 5 minutes until paste is lightly browned. Add lime rind, chiles and scallions. Stir for a further minute then add the beans and coconut milk.

Pour in 1 cup water. Bring to a boil. Lower heat, cover and simmer gently for about 20 minutes until beans are tender. Add salt to taste.

Makes 4 to 6 side-dish servings.

–COCONUT MILK & VEGETABLES–

1½ teaspoons tamarind
2 tablespoons peanut oil
1½ large onion, chopped
2 cloves garlic, chopped
2 fresh red chiles, cored, seeded and chopped
¼ teaspoon ground turmeric
6oz. green beans, cut in 2-inch lengths
1¼ cups coconut milk
8oz. Chinese cabbage, shredded
2 tomatoes, peeled, seeded and chopped
Salt

Soak tamarind in 1½ tablespoons hot water. Strain through fine sieve extracting as much liquid as possible. Reserve liquid.

In a wok or sauté pan, heat oil over medium heat. Add onion, garlic and chiles and cook for about 4 minutes until softened but not colored. Stir in turmeric.

Add beans and ¾ cup coconut milk to pan. Bring to a boil and simmer for 5 minutes. Add cabbage and cook for a further 4 minutes until vegetables are just tender. Stir in tamarind liquid, tomatoes and remaining coconut milk. Heat, stirring, for 1-2 minutes. Season with salt to taste.

Makes 4 to 6 side-dish servings.

──────VEGETABLE STIR-FRY──────

2 tablespoons peanut oil
2 fresh red chiles, cored, seeded and finely chopped
1 (1-inch) piece ginger root, grated
2 cloves garlic, crushed
4oz. each carrots, cut into matchsticks, green beans,
  broccoli florets and baby corn, halved
1 red pepper, cut into fine strips
2 small pak choi, very coarsely chopped
4 scallions, including some green, sliced
1 tablespoon hot curry paste
1¼ cups coconut milk
2 tablespoons Satay Sauce (see page 55)
2 tablespoons soy sauce
1 teaspoon light brown sugar
4 tablespoons chopped fresh cilantro
Whole roasted peanuts, to garnish

In a wok or sauté pan, heat oil. Add chiles, ginger and garlic. Stir-fry for 1 minute. Add carrot, green beans, broccoli, corn, pepper. Over high heat, stir-fry for 3-4 minutes. Stir in pak choi, scallions and curry paste and stir-fry for 1-2 minutes longer.

Stir in coconut milk, satay sauce, soy sauce and sugar. Bring to boil, then simmer 1-2 minutes until vegetables are just tender. Add cilantro then serve garnished with peanuts.

Makes 4 to 6 servings.

——MIXED VEGETABLE SALAD——

3 large carrots, cut into thin 3-inch long sticks
10 yard-long beans, or 3oz. green beans, cut into
   2-inch pieces
½ small cauliflower, divided into florets
1 cucumber, peeled, halved, seeded and cut into matchsticks
8oz. wedge green cabbage, cored and shredded
2 cloves garlic, smashed
6 candlenuts nuts or cashew nuts, chopped
2 fresh red chiles, cored, seeded and chopped
6 shallots, chopped
1½ teaspoon ground turmeric
4 tablespoons vegetable oil
½ cup light brown sugar
¼ cup rice vinegar
Salt
1½oz. roasted unsalted peanuts

Bring a large saucepan of water to a boil.
Add carrots, beans and cauliflower. Simmer
for 2-3 minutes until tender but still crisp.
Add cucumber and cabbage and simmer
1 minute longer. Drain, rinse under cold
running water and drain thoroughly. Put
garlic, nuts, chiles, shallots and turmeric in
a blender. Mix to a paste.

Heat oil in a wok or skillet over medium
heat. Add spice paste and cook, stirring, for
3-5 minutes until slightly thickened and
spices are fragrant. Add sugar, vinegar and
salt to taste. Bring to a boil. Add vegetables
to pan. Stir and toss to coat thoroughly.
Transfer to a bowl. Cover tightly and leave
at room temperature for about 1 hour. To
serve, mound vegetables in a serving dish
and sprinkle peanuts on top.

Makes 8 to 10 servings.

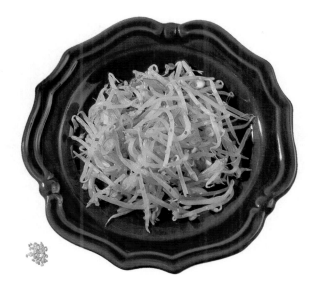

──── BEAN SPROUT SALAD ────

Salt
1¼ lbs. bean sprouts
1 tablespoon sesame seeds
1 fresh red chile, cored, seeded and chopped
2 cloves garlic, finely chopped
2 tablespoons sesame oil
4 scallions including the green, very thinly sliced

Bring a large saucepan of salted water to a boil. Add the bean sprouts all at once. Cover the pan and quickly return to a boil. Uncover the pan and boil for 30 seconds.

Turn bean sprouts into a colander and rinse under running cold water. Press bean sprouts gently to squeeze out surplus water. Transfer bean sprouts to a bowl. Heat a small heavy skillet. Add sesame seeds and dry-fry, stirring, until fragrant and lightly browned. Add to bean sprouts.

Add chile, garlic, sesame oil and scallions to bowl with bean sprouts. Toss to mix ingredients thoroughly.

Makes 4 side-dish servings.

———SPLIT PEA FRITTERS———

8oz. yellow split peas, soaked overnight in cold
  water
3-4 fresh red chiles, cored, seeded and chopped
2 cloves garlic, chopped
2 scallions, sliced
3 tablespoons chopped fresh cilantro
1 teaspoon ground roasted cumin seeds
Large pinch ground turmeric
1 egg, beaten
Salt
Vegetable oil for deep-frying (optional)
Banana leaves (optional)
Dipping Sauce or Spicy Sauce (see page 85), to serve

Drain split peas and put in a saucepan with
1¼ cups water. Bring to a boil. Boil, stirring,
for 10 minutes. Drain. Put in a food
processor with chiles, garlic and scallions.
Mix until coarsely chopped. Add cilantro,
cumin, turmeric, egg and salt to taste and
mix together. Form into about 50 small
balls, pressing mixture firmly together with
your hands. Refrigerate for about 1 hour.

Preheat oven to 450F (230C). Roll patties
in a little oil, put on baking sheets and bake
for 15-17 minutes until golden brown. Turn
over halfway through. Alternatively, heat
oil in a deep-fat fryer to 350F (180C), or
until a cube of bread browns in 30 seconds.
Deep-fry fritters in batches for 2-3 minutes
until golden. Drain on paper towels. Serve
fritters hot on banana leaves, if liked,
accompanied by the dipping sauce of your
choice.

Makes about 50 (6 servings).

SWEET POTATO RINGS

18oz. sweet potatoes, peeled and cubed
2 tablespoons vegetable oil, plus oil for frying
1 onion, finely chopped
2 cloves garlic, finely crushed
1 fresh red chile, cored, seeded and chopped
1 tablespoon curry powder
1 egg, beaten
Salt and freshly ground black pepper
1 cup all-purpose flour
Dried breadcrumbs
Cilantro sprigs, to garnish

Steam sweet potato cubes for 6-8 minutes until tender. Pass through a vegetable mill into a bowl, or mash thoroughly.

Meanwhile, in a wok or skillet, heat oil and fry onion, garlic and chile until onion is lightly colored. Stir in curry powder for 1 minute. Add onion mixture to sweet potato with egg, and salt and pepper to taste. Beat together until evenly mixed then stir in flour to bind together; if mixture is too soft, add a little more flour. Leave to cool then refrigerate for at least 1 hour, if necessary.

Using oiled hands, form mixture into balls about 1½ inches in diameter. Press lightly to flatten into cakes. With the floured end of a wooden spoon press through the center of each cake to make a ring. Thoroughly coat rings in breadcrumbs, pressing them in. Chill for at least 1 hour. Heat ½-inch depth of oil in a skillet and fry rings until crisp and golden. Using a spatula, transfer to paper towels to drain. Serve warm, garnished with cilantro sprigs.

Makes 4 servings.

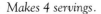

VEGETARIAN STIR-FRY

8 dried Chinese black mushrooms
8oz. firm tofu, rinsed
1 tablespoon cornstarch
3 tablespoons peanut oil
3 cloves garlic, finely chopped
1 fresh red chile, cored, seeded and chopped
8oz. yard-long beans or green beans, cut into
   2-inch lengths
2 carrots, thinly sliced diagonally
½ cauliflower, divided into florets
6oz. snow peas
3 tablespoons soy sauce
2 teaspoons dark sesame oil
2 teaspoons light brown sugar

Soak mushrooms in 115ml (4fl oz/½ cup) warm water for 30 minutes. Drain through muslin; reserve liquid. Slice mushroom caps and discard stalks. Pat tofu dry. Cut tofu into 2.5cm (1inch cubes. Put cornstarch on a plate and dip tofu into to coat evenly; press cornstarch in firmly. In a wok or skillet, heat oil; add tofu and fry for 6-8 minutes until browned on all sides. Using a slotted spoon transfer to paper towels to drain.

Add garlic, chile, beans, carrots and cauliflower to pan and stir-fry for 1 minute. Add snow peas and stir-fry for a minute longer. Add black mushrooms and the reserved mushroom liquid. Stir-fry for about 5 minutes until vegetables are tender. Stir soy sauce, sesame oil and sugar into vegetables. Add fried tofu and toss gently until hot and coated with the liquid.

Makes 4 servings.

NOODLES WITH TOFU

6 oz. thin Chinese egg noodles
2 tablespoons vegetable oil
6 shallots, finely chopped
3 cloves garlic, finely crushed
2 fresh red chiles, cored, seeded and chopped
5 eggs
8 oz. firm tofu, cut into thin strips
2 tablespoons soy sauce
¼ cup rice vinegar
1½ tablespoons light brown sugar
Salt
Grated rind of ½ lime
2 scallions, white and green parts, thinly sliced
3 tablespoons chopped fresh cilantro
4 oz. bean sprouts

Cook noodles according to instructions on package. Meanwhile, in a wok or sauté pan over medium heat, heat oil. Add shallots, garlic and chiles and stir-fry until the shallots are lightly browned.

Break all the eggs into the pan. Stir for 1 minute, breaking up the yolks. Add the tofu, soy sauce, vinegar, sugar and salt to taste. Toss the ingredients together until the eggs are set. Drain noodles. Toss with egg and tofu mixture, the lime rind, scallions and cilantro. Scatter bean sprouts on top.

Makes 4 servings.

TOFU SALAD

8oz. firm tofu
3 large carrots, cut into thin 3-inch long sticks
10 yard-long beans, or 3oz. green beans, cut into
  2-inch pieces
1 cucumber, peeled, halved, seeded and cut into matchsticks
8oz. bean sprouts
PEANUT DRESSING
2 cloves garlic, smashed
6 shallots, chopped
2 fresh red chiles, cored, seeded and chopped
3oz. roasted unsalted peanuts
3 tablespoons peanut oil
2 tablespoons light brown sugar
4 tablespoons rice vinegar
1 tablespoon soy sauce
Juice of 1 lime

Half-fill a saucepan with water. Bring to a
boil. Add tofu and simmer, turning once, for
10 minutes. Drain, cool on paper towels,
then cut into ½-inch cubes. Bring a large
saucepan of water to a boil. Add carrots and
beans. Simmer for 2 minutes until tender
but still crisp. Add cucumber and simmer 1
minute more. Drain, rinse under cold
running water and drain thoroughly. To
make dressing, put garlic, shallots, chiles
and peanuts in a blender. Mix to a paste.

Heat oil in a wok or skillet over medium
heat. Add peanut paste and cook, stirring,
for 3-5 minutes until slightly thickened and
fragrant. Add sugar, vinegar, soy sauce, lime
juice and 4 tablespoons water. Bring to a
boil. Remove pan from heat. Arrange bean
sprouts on a serving plate. Top with other
vegetables and tofu. Spoon some dressing
over. Cover and chill for 1 hour. Serve
remaining dressing separately.

Makes 4 servings.

—DIPPING SAUCE & SPICY SAUCE—

DIPPING SAUCE
1 garlic clove, crushed
Salt
4 tablespoons light soy sauce
2½ tablespoons lime juice
1 tablespoon very finely sliced scallion
1 teaspoon light brown sugar
1 or 2 drops of chile sauce

Mash the garlic clove with a very small pinch of salt. In a small dish, put garlic, soy sauce, lime juice, scallion and sugar. Add chile sauce to taste. Stir before serving.

Makes 4 servings.

SPICY SAUCE
4 dried red chiles, cored, seeded and chopped
6 tablespoons peanut oil
4 shallots, finely chopped
8 cloves garlic, finely chopped
1 medium ripe tomato, coarsely chopped
1 teaspoon ground coriander seeds
1 teaspoon ground cumin seeds
1 teaspoon light brown sugar

In a small bowl, soak chiles in 3 tablespoons hot water for 15 minutes. Drain and reserve. Heat oil in a skillet over medium-low heat. Add shallots and fry until softened.

Add garlic, tomato, coriander seeds, cumin seeds and sugar to pan. Bring to a boil, then simmer for 3-4 minutes. Pour into a fine sieve placed over a bowl. Press through as much of the contents of sieve as possible. Cover liquid and keep in a refrigerator until required.

Makes 6 servings.

SHRIMP PASTE RELISH

8 fresh red chiles, cored, seeded and chopped
1 tablespoon shrimp paste, roasted (see page 10)
2½ tablespoons lime juice

In a mortar or small bowl, pound chiles with a pestle or end of a rolling pin. Add shrimp paste and pound thoroughly.

Gradually add lime juice, using pestle or end of rolling pin to work lime juice into pounded chiles.

Serve relish in a nonreactive bowl.

Makes 4 to 6 servings.

——————COCONUT SAMBAL——————

2 oz. dried shrimps
6 oz. shredded coconut
2 fresh red chiles, cored, seeded and chopped
1 small onion, chopped
2 cloves garlic, smashed
1 stalk lemon grass, chopped
3 tablespoons vegetable oil

In a mortar or small bowl, pound shrimps with a pestle or end of a rolling pin, until fairly fine. Add coconut and work in lightly.

Put chiles, onion, garlic and lemon grass in a blender. Mix to a paste.

Heat oil in a wok or small skillet over medium heat. Add spice paste and fry, stirring, for about 3 minutes until very fragrant. Add coconut mixture and fry until coconut is crisp and golden. Transfer to a small serving bowl and leave until cold. Store in a covered glass jar in the refrigerator.

Makes 6 servings.

FRESH MINT SAMBAL

2 oz. mint leaves
1 (½-inch) piece of ginger root, coarsely chopped
1 small onion, coarsely chopped
4 tablespoons lime juice
Salt

Put mint, ginger, onion and lime juice in a blender. Mix to a paste. Season with salt to taste.

Transfer sambal to a serving small bowl. Serve sambal with curries or Curry Puffs (see page 18).

Makes 1 cup.

–CUCUMBER & PINEAPPLE SALAD–

1¼ cups peeled chopped pineapple
6 oz. cucumber, peeled
2 shallots, thinly sliced
½-1 thin fresh red chile, cored, seeded and thinly
  sliced
15-20 mint leaves, torn into small pieces
2 tablespoons lime juice
1¼ teaspoons light brown sugar
Salt

Cut pineapple and cucumber into about 2-inch long strips. Put into a nonreactive bowl.

Add shallots, chile, mint leaves, lime juice and sugar to bowl. Stir together.

Season salad with salt to taste. Adjust levels of chile, mint, lime juice and sugar to taste if necessary.

Makes 4 to 6 servings.

MANGO CHUTNEY

4 lbs. green mangoes, peeled and cubed
2 limes, sliced into semi-circles
3 fresh red chiles, cored, seeded and finely chopped
3 cups+2 tablespoons white wine vinegar
1 tablespoon ground toasted cardamom seeds
1 teaspoon ground toasted cumin seeds
1 teaspoon ground turmeric
1½ teaspoons salt
1 lb. light brown sugar

Put mangoes, limes, chiles and vinegar into a nonreactive pan. Bring to a boil then lower heat and simmer, uncovered, for 10-15 minutes until mangoes are just tender.

Add spices, salt and sugar. Stir until sugar has dissolved, then increase heat and bring to a boil. Lower heat again and simmer, uncovered, for 50-60 minutes, stirring occasionally, until most of the liquid has evaporated and the chutney is quite thick.

Ladle chutney into hot, very clean jars. Cover top of each jar of chutney with a disc of waxed paper, waxed side down. Close jars with nonreactive lids. Leave chutney for 1 month before using.

Makes about 3 lbs.

QUICK MIXED PICKLE

2 fresh red chiles, cored, seeded and chopped
7 shallots, 5 chopped, 2 left whole
6 cloves garlic, 3 chopped, 3 left whole
1 (1½-inch) piece ginger root, grated
6oz. cauliflower florets
4 small carrots, cut into fine sticks
6oz. unpeeled cucumber, cut into fine sticks
3 tablespoons vegetable oil
1 tablespoon curry powder
½ teaspoon each black mustard seeds and ground
  turmeric
2 teaspoons light brown sugar
4 tablespoons rice vinegar
Salt
1 tablespoon sesame oil
1 tablespoon toasted sesame seeds

Put chiles, chopped shallots and chopped
garlic and ¾ ginger in a blender. Add
1 tablespoon water and mix to a paste. Bring
a large saucepan of water to a boil. Add
cauliflower and carrots. Quickly return to a
boil. After 30 seconds add cucumber and
boil for about 3 seconds. Turn into a
colander and rinse under running cold
water.

Heat oil in a large saucepan. Add spice
paste and fry for 1 minute. Add whole
shallots and whole garlic and remaining
ginger. Stir-fry for 30 seconds. Reduce heat
to medium low. Stir in curry powder,
mustard seeds, turmeric and sugar. Add
vinegar, blanched vegetables and 1½
teaspoons salt. Bring to a boil. Remove from
heat and stir in sesame oil and sesame seeds.
Cool then ladle into a warm jar. Cover with
nonreactive lid. Refrigerate when cold.

Makes 4 cups.

COCONUT CUSTARDS

1 pandan leaf (optional)
2½ cups coconut milk
3 whole eggs
3 egg yolks
About ½ cup sugar
½ cup light cream

Run the tines of a fork through the pandan leaf, if using. Tie in a knot. Pour coconut milk into a nonstick saucepan, add pandan leaf and bring to just below a simmer. Remove from heat, cover and leave for 20 minutes. Discard pandan leaf.

Preheat oven to 350F (180C). Reheat (or heat) coconut milk to a boil. In a bowl, whisk together eggs, egg yolks and sugar until evenly blended. Slowly pour in coconut milk, whisking constantly. Add cream.

Strain into a pitcher and pour into 8 ramekin dishes. Set ramekins in a roasting pan and pour boiling water into pan to come halfway up sides of ramekins. Cook in oven for 20-25 minutes until a skewer inserted in center comes out clean. Remove ramekins from pan and leave to cool. Refrigerate until chilled.

Makes 8 servings.

—PINEAPPLE WITH COCONUT—

½ cup sugar
1 (1½-inch) piece ginger root, grated
½ cup light brown sugar
12 thin slices fresh pineapple
3-4 tablespoons coconut flakes, toasted

Put sugar, ginger and light brown sugar in a heavy-bottom saucepan. Stir in 1⅔ cups water. Heat gently, stirring with a wooden spoon, until sugars have melted. Bring to a boil. Simmer until reduced by about a third.

Remove cores from slices of pineapple using a small sharp knife or a small cookie cutter. Strain syrup over pineapple rings and leave to cool. Cover and chill.

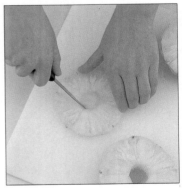

To serve, lay 2 pineapple rings on each plate. Spoon some of the syrup over and scatter the toasted coconut flakes on top.

Makes 6 servings.

──MALAYSIAN FRUIT SALAD──

¼ cup light brown sugar
Grated rind and juice of 1 lime
1 small pineapple, peeled, cored and cubed
1½ lbs. lychees, peeled, halved and pitted
3 ripe mangoes, peeled, pitted and chopped
1 papaya, peeled, seeded and chopped

Put sugar, lime rind and juice and ⅔ cup water in a saucepan. Heat gently, stirring with a wooden spoon, until sugar has dissolved.

Heat syrup to boiling point, then simmer for 1 minute. Remove from heat and leave to cool.

Put pineapple, lychees, mangoes and papaya in a serving dish. Pour over cool syrup. Cover dish with plastic wrap and put in the refrigerator to chill.

Makes 4 servings.

SAGO PUDDING

2 cups milk or water
6oz. sago, rinsed
1½ cups coconut milk
¼ cup light cream
SYRUP
⅔ cup palm sugar or brown sugar
small piece fresh ginger root or lemon grass
1 pandan leaf (optional)

In a saucepan, bring milk or water to a boil. Add sago, stir and simmer for 10-15 minutes, stirring occasionally, until tender. Cool slightly and spoon into individual glass dishes. Cool completely, then refrigerate.

To make syrup, in a saucepan, gently heat sugar with ¾ cup water and the ginger or lemon grass, and pandan leaf, if using, stirring with a wooden spoon until sugar has dissolved. Bring to a boil. Simmer for a few minutes until syrup thickens. Strain and leave to cool.

Mix together coconut milk and cream, then chill. To serve, pour creamy coconut milk around edges of sago puddings. Make a well in the center of the puddings and pour in some of the syrup.

Makes 6 servings.

INDEX

Aromatic Chicken, 47

Beansprout Salad, 79
Beef in Chile Sauce, 56
Braised Chicken with
    Spices, 44
Broiled Chicken Skewers, 29

Chicken & Noodle Soup, 15
Chicken & Pineapple
    Curry, 45
Chicken & Shrimp Noodles,
    65
Chicken in Spiced Sauce, 43
Chicken with Rice, 52
Coconut Curried Fish, 31
Coconut Custards, 92
Coconut Milk &
    Vegetables, 76
Coconut Sambal, 87
Crisp Fish with Turmeric, 32
Cucumber & Pineapple Salad,
    89
Curried Coconut Beef, 58
Curry Puffs, 18

Devil's Curry, 46
Dim Sum, 26
Dipping Sauce, 85
"Dry" Beef with Coconut, 57

Fish Steaks with Chile, 37
Fragrant Shrimp, 40
Fresh Mint Sambal, 88
Fried Noodles with Crab, 67
Fried Rice Noodles, 62

Ginger & Soy Roast Chicken,
    51
Green Beans in Spiced Sauce,
    75

Laksa Lemak, 12
Lamb Curry, 59

Malay Chicken, 48
Malaysian Fried Rice, 69
Malaysian Fruit Salad, 94
Malaysian Spring Rolls, 22
Mango Chutney, 90
Marinated Broiled Fish, 34
Mild Fish Curry, 30
Mixed Satay, 54
Mixed Vegetable Salad, 78
Mussels in Hot Spicy Sauce,
    39

Nonya Chicken, 49
Nonya Packages, 28
Noodles with Tofu, 83
Noodles with Beansprouts, 64
Noodles with Fish, 66
Noodles with Peanut Sauce,
    63

Okra in Spice Sauce, 74

Penang Hot-sour Soup, 13
Pineapple with Coconut, 93
Poh Piah, 24
Pork with Tamarind, 53

Quick Mixed Pickle, 91

Rice with Lemon Grass, 68

Sago Pudding, 95
Sarawak Marinated Fish, 36
Satay Sauce, 55
Seafood & Coconut
    Soup, 16
Shrimp Paste Relish, 86
Shrimp Balls, 20
Shrimp Kebabs, 42
Shrimp Omelet, 21
Shrimp Robed in Spices, 41
Singapore Steamboat, 60
Spiced Chicken, 50
Spiced Fish in Banana Leaves,
    33
Spiced Grilled Squash, 71
Spiced Rice, 70
Spiced Sweet & Sour
    Fish, 35
Spicy Sauce, 85
Spicy Spare Ribs, 25
Spinach with Sesame, 73
Split Pea Fritters, 80
Stir-fried Sugar Snap Peas, 72
Sweet & Sour Fish, 38
Sweet Potato Rings, 81

Tofu Salad, 84
Tofu Soup, 17

Vegetable Stir-fry, 77
Vegetarian Stir-fry, 82

Wonton Soup,
    14